The
Customer
SHOUTS
Back!™

10 Big Changes You Need to Make
To Win Their Lifetime Loyalty

ROSS SHAFER

First published by Dog Ear Publishing
4010 W. 86th Street, Ste H
Indianapolis, IN 46268
www.dogearpublishing.net

ISBN: 978-1-4276-0783-6

This book is printed on acid-free paper.

Printed in the United States of America

This book is for my mother; Lois Shafer.
You have been a lifelong role model
for empathy and humanity.
I've never heard you be a difficult customer.
And, regardless of how you were treated, you
always left clerks, salespeople, and
service providers with a smile on their faces.
I wish more of that had rubbed off on me.

TABLE OF CONTENTS

SECTION THREE

10 BIG CHANGES YOU NEED TO MAKE IF YOU WANT THEIR LIFETIME LOYALTY

SECTION FOUR

LEARN FROM ORGANIZATIONS WHO ARE GETTING IT RIGHT

INTRODUCTION

It has only taken our culture 50 years to destroy customer service.

This book is about what caused the destruction—and how to fix it.

For years, customers have been trying to tell us how to stop this decaying problem but we haven't been listening.

Now, they are *Shouting Back*; refusing to spend money with the people and companies who mistreat them.

You know the kind of mistreatment I'm talking about. When you leave your job, *you* become the customer. And, you've probably left a recent purchase thinking, "Why doesn't anyone say, *Thank You,* anymore"—"Why are people so *rude* to me"—"Why would a clerk talk on the phone with their friends...when I'm standing there trying to spend money with them!?" And, the perennial, "Don't they know they wouldn't have a job if it wasn't for customers like me?"

Even though we spend some 60 billion dollars a year training and re-training employees, customer service is at an all time low. If we are spending so much money on training, shouldn't service be stellar? Aren't managers supposed to be more enlightened?

A lot of people look to our company for those answers.

Since 1995, our company has written and produced (14) human resource training films; on the subject of customer service and leadership. Every year, I speak to 100+ corporations on customer service. I am hired by the managers who craft their "customer mission statements" and I talk to the front line folks who are in charge of executing the "mission."

These organizations agree that service is their weakest component. But when I talk to the managers, I find that they are trying to put a band-aid on the wrong things. They're instructing employees to smile and to repeat the customer's name; thinking those behaviors build customer loyalty.

They don't.

Those "remedies" are only a topical ointment for a systemic disease that is now poised to cripple our global economy.

If you suspect I'm sensationalizing the impact of bad customer service to sell books, consider this:

At this writing, the ACSI (American Customer Satisfaction Index) clearly indicates that customer satisfaction is slipping in all areas of commerce.

The ACSI is a highly respected (and exhaustive) survey conducted by the University of Michigan; School of Business. They cover all retail, service, and manufacturing categories. Using their 100 point scale, they identify customer service trends as well as the specific culprits who cause the Index to go up or down. A low ACSI rating has become significant enough to affect stock prices. A lower capital value can affect your IRA, your company's future, your impending bonus, and even your next month's paycheck.

Professor Claes Fornell, Director, National Quality Research Center, Stephen M. Ross Business School at the University of Michigan, reported that bad customer service means consumers stop spending.

That's really bad news for you, your business, and the world. Fornell says,

> "Customer dissatisfaction with the quality goods
> and services offered in the marketplace is more
> than a nuisance. The US economy is heavily

dependent on increases in consumer spending. Such increases are hard to come by when consumers become less satisfied...The Index now stands at 73.6—dropping nearly 1% compared with the third quarter."

Fornell says just because your company is growing, you could be in for a rude awakening. When a company expands too quickly, one of the first things to suffer is customer satisfaction.

"A major cause of the plunge in customer satisfaction appears to be problems with servicing a growing volume of shoppers. While high levels of customer satisfaction typically lead to company growth, it is not always the case that business growth leads to satisfied customers. In many cases, the opposite is true. Through heavy discounting, the holiday season did bring in more buyers for both traditional and online retailers. But because some companies also cut costs, resources to serve the increasing demand were sometimes lacking, resulting in crowding, longer lines, and slower service."

And, he paints a dismal picture for the future.

"...Chances are that this will happen again. In addition to the negative financial consequences for companies with a less satisfied customer base, the drop in ACSI is not a good sign for the economy. It does not help trade or budget deficits. Demand for domestic goods and services are not likely to benefit, especially since customer

satisfaction appears stronger for many retailers selling imported goods. Gross Domestic Product (GDP) growth will also be more difficult if consumers reduce their rate of spending. There will be more pressure on the dollar and higher interest rates as a result. Higher rates, in turn, don't encourage companies to devote more resources to satisfying customers. As interest rates rise, the value of the returning customer diminishes because future income streams become more heavily discounted."

Let me translate: Bad customer service can put the world in serious financial peril! Bad service leads to lower spending. Lower spending means lower profits. Lower profits mean companies will spend less on the customer satisfaction component.

The hopeful news in their research is that better customer service can actually reverse this deadly downward spiral.

If what we, as managers and trainers, have been doing hasn't worked, then what's the solution?

In 1998, we got close.

Back then, one of our most successful films was titled, *The Customer Talks Back.*

It was successful because we didn't write it.

We simply took a camera out on the streets and inside shopping malls. Then, we let people tell us what they liked and disliked about customer service. Their answers were candid and pure. Their memories were sharp and their emotions (from the experience) were vivid and unforgiving. Customers told us they wanted five things.

- A Smile

- Eye Contact

- Respect for their Money and Time

- Just Enough Attention

- Well Informed Sales Staff

But even though we'd faithfully recorded the customer's exact complaint, we hadn't fully captured the customer's *emotions* triggered by their dissatisfaction.

So, in order to be relevant and fresh, we knew we needed to either do hidden camera work (which we didn't do) or "drill down" in an anonymous way—adopt a fly-on-the-customer's-wall approach to discover what customers were really thinking and feeling.

In a new round of research, we carefully examined 1,000 customer complaints (from 2004 & 2005). This time we paid close attention to the complaints that spoke to the customer's feelings of desperation, hopelessness, frustration, and anxiety.

And man, did they shout back!

To the core question of "value," customers said they felt "cheated" and "lied to" when the experience didn't live up to the promise made by the advertising. Conversely, they felt "loved" when they found a company that made them feel wanted and delivered on its promises.

This was to be the starting point for the solution.

It is impossible to create customer loyalty when the customer leaves you feeling rejected, unimportant, and/or disliked. Repeated bad feelings create enemies. As you know, enemies are (traditionally) not very loyal.

But to fix it, we felt we needed to know how and why businesses have come to treat people so badly in the first place. Why is this damaging attitude so pervasive?

In this book, we'll examine the significant events in our culture that have contributed to the death of customer service—and how we have inadvertently initiated a dangerous shift in human nature.

Then, we'll propose (10) specific changes you can make that will reverse the cycle and resurrect customer service.

Incidentally, you'll make lots of money in the process.

If you *love* your customers, they will love you back and you won't have to compete on price. Competing on price alone is a battle you can't win. You will never beat Wal*Mart on price and you can't beat countries like China on cost. The only competitive advantage left to you is to whip your competition at *customer relations*. Instead of "training" people to smile, let's teach them how to think with their hearts. Let's teach managers and employees to become customer "psychologists." Teach them to 'read' people. Attune them to listen to the *feelings* behind the customer's words. Encourage employees to create customer loyalty through a true *emotional connection*.

The customer is *shouting back*. If you learn to *really* listen to them—and respond with humanity—they will reward you with a lifetime of loyalty.

CUSTOMERS ARE SHOUTING BACK!

CHAPTER 1

YOUR CUSTOMERS ARE SHOUTING BACK

Customers aren't just complaining. They are speaking in angry voices and they are closing their big fat wallets. You've probably exchanged shopping nightmares with your friends at work.

But, when customer-service-horror-stories became the hot topic at my wife's birthday party, I knew our public consciousness had reached a boiling point.

Right in the middle of scooping a beautifully chubby corn chip through a seven-layer dip, tales of bad customer complaints started bubbling to the surface. Picture yourself in mid-dip when your best friend interrupts to say,

> *"Last Saturday I went to Lowe's (home improvement center) and tried to get some help from this guy. But he was on the phone with another employee—going over a scheduling conflict. Instead of putting that employee on hold,*

they argued back and forth about who would work which hours. I finally butted in and said, 'Excuse me, I need to exchange this broken lamp.' The clerk totally ignored me and kept talking to his friend. So, I had another clerk call the manager. When the manager showed up, I told him what happened. The little jerk lied to the manager saying he was talking to a customer. I was infuriated. I called him a liar and threw the lamp box on the counter and walked out."

That prompted this story:

"I know what you mean. I went to Home Depot because I wanted to buy some patio furniture. I knew what I wanted but I couldn't find anyone to sell it to me. So, I figured I'd load it on a cart myself. I only saw their little baskets so I went outside to see if I could find a big flat cart. No luck. So, I asked this young guy if he could find a flat cart for me. He said, "You'll have to look in the parking lot." I told him I was just out there. He looked at me and said, "Well if I go out there it will be the same as you looking. I can't do any better than that." I bought the furniture somewhere else."

Somebody else jumped in to switch the subject away from home improvement to...tanning salons.

"I went to this place called Club Tan (indoor tanning salon) and asked if I could get a three-month tanning package ($280) to share with my husband. The girl behind the counter was so rude and told me they didn't have shared packages. I asked why not. She said, "It's our

policy and it doesn't matter how many times
people ask for it we are not changing our policy."
So I bought a tanning package two blocks away."

Everyone looked at me like it was *my* fault. After all, we produce customer service training films, right?

I was rescued when somebody said, *"Isn't that what they pay HR managers for?"*

Another person chimed in, *"I don't think managers know what's really happening on the sales floor, these days."*

Well, it really doesn't matter whose fault it was. The customer isn't happy and they want some big changes.

WE NEEDED A "DEEPER DIVE"

In a fresh round of research, we examined 1,000 independently written customer complaints filed throughout 2004 and 2005. We found them on open forum web sites like, www.complaints.com, www.my3cents.com, www.clik2complaints.com, www.thesqueakywheel.com, www.fightback.com, www.trading-standards.co.uk, and the latest web community phenomenon; blogs. What fascinated us was that these "complainers" weren't writing letters to the company who wronged them. They had already tried that route and couldn't get anyone to help them. In their abject dissatisfaction, these customers wrote letters to other web sites and customer-service-abused people. They were hoping that someone in cyber space would help them resolve their issue. And, to add a quantitative factor, we consulted research done by the Gallup Organization (some 15 million customer responses) as well as published data collected from J.D. Power and Associates.

Needless to say, the responses propped our eyes (and hearts) wide open.

PEOPLE ARE FAR MORE "EMOTIONAL" THAN WE THOUGHT

The startling element we uncovered was the fervent *emotional impact* the customer felt before, during, and after the transaction. In our 1998 film, *The Customer Talks Back,* customers told us what was wrong but they didn't always articulate the *emotions* behind how they felt. We accepted that because, as unbiased advocates for the customer, we assumed the customer was always right.

That was our first mistake.

Then, we made the naïve assumption that the customer was confident, collected, and in control.

Our second mistake.

Customers weren't just complaining. They had specific *feelings* associated with bad customer service.

When a person doesn't smile at a customer, they *feel disliked.* If the sales associate doesn't make eye contact, they *feel unimportant.* When a clerk doesn't acknowledge a customer, they *feel rejected.* If a clerk uses foul language within earshot of the customer, the customer *feels embarrassed, insulted,* and sometimes *angry.*

PUT YOURSELF IN *THEIR* EMOTIONS

When you love someone more than they love you, you feel "off balance" and vulnerable. Your emotions live just under your skin because you're afraid you could lose them and get hurt, right?

Now, imagine how vulnerable you might feel if you were buying a new house and had to sit down and sign a two-inch-tall stack of unfamiliar papers. You wouldn't be very comfortable, would you? Do you read every word of the molecule-sized print—or do you have to trust your mortgage lender and realtor to cover your @$$?

How vulnerable would you feel if you found out you were overdrawn at the bank? And, you're not sure if it was your mistake or theirs? How would it feel if you had to go into the bank branch to cover the shortage? Most customers in that situation said they felt embarrassed and humiliated.

How vulnerable do you feel when the auto mechanic tells you it will cost $1,200 to get your car back on the road. Do you know if he's right? Are you a car expert? Or, do you have to trust the mechanic? You feel anxious and helpless, don't you?

Curt Coffman, author of *Follow This Path* and co-author of *First, Break All The Rules,* posed this question to me, *"Would a customer be a customer if they could meet their own needs? NO!"*

Curt is right. Otherwise, we would be independent transaction machines like the ATM.

> *SIDE NOTE: ATM's have become popular because the ATM machine puts you in control. You can withdraw and deposit money on your own time schedule. It's no surprise why other electronic kiosks for airline tickets, groceries, hotels, and home improvement items have caught on. Self service kiosks make us feel like successful partners in the purchase process. And, we don't have to suffer any emotional rejection from a neglectful salesperson.*

The truth is that customers *do* need you—and they don't like needing you because when you need someone you are in a very weakened and vulnerable state.

So, let's look at who wrote the complaint letters and why?

CHAPTER 2

WOMEN WERE THE BIGGEST COMPLAINERS

What may surprise (half of you) is that 86% of the complaints were written by women.

Don't jump to conclusions.

Women wrote the most complaints NOT because women are prone to complaining...but rather because...

WOMEN BUY EVERYTHING!

I told the following joke to a group of high powered telecom executives,

"Women's magazines not only focus on developing and sustaining relationships—but also devote a lot of pages to hair and fashion. You see, women really care about how they present themselves. In fact, the women in this room are wearing clothes that were made this year!"

Management guru, Tom Peters, was in the crowd and really liked that joke. Then, he told me at the break, *"Women have another unique trait...they buy everything!"*

He's right.

Take a look at these statistics from his book, *Reimagine.* Women make...

83% of all Consumer purchases.

94% of Home Furnishing purchases

92% of the Vacation Decision purchases

91% of new Home Buying purchases

70% of Small Business Loans and start ups

80% of Do-It-Yourself home projects

80% of the Healthcare Decisions

89% of the Bank Accounts

67% of all Household Investment Decisions

68% of all Automobile purchases.

And what they don't buy, they influence. In the typically male dominated realm of buying computers and consumer electronics, women still make 51% of the decisions. You guys may think you are buying your favorite big screen TV, but I'll bet your wife is telling you where it will go and she'll dictate the cabinet color!

Women are a powerful force!

You want them on your side.

The women who wrote the complaint letters were articulate, understanding, and patient. They would have been willing to work things out if someone would have just listened and been collaborative in trying to find a solution.

Barbara Pease, who wrote the book, *Men Don't Listen & Women Can't Read Maps*, sizes the sexes up like this:

"Boys compete. Girls cooperate. Boys like things. Women like people. Men hide their emotions. Women talk emotively."

In fact, the complaint letters we read were filled with emotional remarks, from women, like:

"I felt totally rejected."

"It was such a painful experience."

"The sales girl made me feel like an idiot."

"He talked to me like I was a child."

"I will never go through that kind of humiliation again."

"I have never felt so helpless in my life."

Female buying power cannot be ignored. In their book, *Trading Up*, Michael Silverstein and Neil Fiske describe how the purchasing landscape has changed.

"Just as important as the increased wealth of Americans is the newly dominant role played by women, both as consumers and as influencers of consumption. The percentage of women in the workforce has risen steadily and dramatically over the past four decades, and the percentage of married couples with a wife in the paid labor force has nearly doubled. Not only are women working, they are earning higher salaries than ever before; nearly a quarter of married women make more money than their husbands do.

Women feel they have the right to spend it on themselves."

Since women are such powerful purchasing agents, shouldn't we be paying more attention to their emotional feelings?

Uh...Yes!

It doesn't matter what industry you can name, cooperation, emotional reactions, and liking people are the key ingredients to improving not only customer service, but harmony with all other life forms. Women "get" the emotional connection required to sustain purchasing loyalty.

WOMEN NAMED NAMES

Women were also fearless when it came to "ratting out" a wrongdoer.

They weren't ashamed to stand up and demand accountability. The customers who wrote the complaint letters signed their names, supplied their email addresses, and weren't afraid to name the companies and the specific individual(s) who mistreated them. These complainers wanted somebody to be accountable.

WHAT DID THEY COMPLAIN ABOUT?

We read letters from the United States to Indonesia. From Africa to India. We threw out some of the letters because the translations were unintelligible or they rambled incoherently. We focused on the complaints that sounded honorable, detailed, truly frustrated, and totally vulnerable. Some of the letters had multiple emotional responses. But, we counted each complaint as an individual response—in the categories dictated by the customer; not by us.

Keep in mind that 100% of the complaints came from unhappy customers. The following statistics describe the source(s) of their unhappiness.

34% FELT CHEATED & LIED TO:

The largest number of dissatisfied customers felt cheated, lied to, or suckered by the purchase of a service or product. When the product or service did not meet their "expectation" or didn't match the advertised "promise"—they felt duped. The "duped" feeling ranged from anger—to frustration—to stupid. This group complained that regardless of price, they expected a certain level of quality and service that was sorely lacking.

23% SAID THE COMPANY TOOK NO RESPONSIBILITY:

The second largest number of complaints speaks to the accountability and empowerment issues. Customers said the company flat out took no responsibility for their problem. The company also took no responsibility for following up with them; after promising they would. Complainers also stated that employees made no effort to solve the problem themselves—but rather deferred to a superior or blankly recited, "It's not our policy." If the company *did* return calls, many customers were made to feel stupid, silly, dumb, and ultimately blamed for the problem.

18% FELT IGNORED:

A significant number of the complaints came from customers who felt totally ignored when they had a beef with the company. They wanted to resolve the issue but were made to feel unimportant and "invisible." They characterized ignoring behavior as "making a personal phone call in front of me," "doing busy work and not even acknowledging I existed," "putting me on hold and forgetting about me," and "giving their friends and co-workers attention while I am standing there trying to buy something."

10% SAID THEY HAD TO DEAL WITH INCOMETENCE:

Customers felt frustrated with the company's basic employee incompetence in dealing with problems. They were appalled that the company didn't use common sense and fairness to resolve their "small issue." They frequently commented that the company did a horrible job of running the basic sell, deliver, support, and guarantee process.

SIDE NOTE: This means that even though Mr. or Mrs. Customer isn't a high paid "operations consultant," he/she can still identify when the business operations grind the transaction to a halt. Every manager should be held accountable for making the operations run smoothly. And, some are. Recently, When Carly Fiorina, CEO of

Hewlett Packard, was let go in February 2005,
New HP Chairman, Patricia Dean, told USA Today
writers Michelle Kessler and Jon Swartz that
Fiorina's downfall was, "her inability to handle
everyday operational issues—the nuts and bolts
of selling computers."

9% WERE TREATED RUDELY:

Customers said that they were treated rudely by an employee and often by the manager or supervisor. They complained about a lack of basic respect and manners. They described rudeness as, "dismissing my concerns," "she was condescending toward m," and "he got in my face and called me a liar."

7% PAID FOR SERVICES THEY DID NOT RECEIVE:

A very small percentage of companies actually seemed to bilk the customer out of their money.

MULTI-COMPLAINING

We also found that complainers didn't just limit their complaint to one of the single categories above. Of the people who complained about being lied to or cheated, 87% of that group also said the company took no responsibility, ignored them at some point, was incompetent, and treated them rudely. Poor customer service "behaviors" went from bad to worse.

ARE COMPLAINERS LOST TO YOU FOREVER?

Shockingly, the answer is, "No."

In a separate survey, we wanted to know what percentage of customers would stop buying from a company as a result of poor treatment. Only 12% said they would *never* go back. That means 88% of badly treated customers could be salvaged. And, these customers have given you clear instructions on how to restore the relationship; even when there is a serious problem. They want you to...

1. Be accountable for you the quality of your goods and services.

2. Take responsibility for the problem.

3. Be Competent.

4. Treat customers with empathy and understanding.

Even at your worst, there seems to be an overwhelming amount of resilience in trying to do business with you. Of the 12% who said they would never come back, only 3% threatened to file a lawsuit if they didn't get their issue resolved. But, please don't assess that 3% as an acceptable loss. They are still emotional human beings who can be highly unpredictable and irrational if you don't satisfy them.

SOME COMPLAINERS WANTED REVENGE.

When people feel cheated or lied to—and no one apologizes—their emotions *can* run high. Here are a few excerpts that were suitable for print.

"Now I know why the phone company customer service people use an alias. Because they know

we would hunt them down and make them pay for causing us so much harassment and money."

"It's quite clear that they set a trap to cheat us out of our money. Next time I see that clerk I am going to set my own trap."

"I have a rule. You lie to me once and I will forgive you. Lie to me twice and you better walk on the other side of the street."

"I don't have time for swindlers and snake oil salesmen. But I do have time to eliminate them from ever cheating anybody else again."

These days, it can be fatal mistake to underestimate the power of a customer's emotions when they feel "wronged." You never know if (or when) one of them will hit their breaking point.

In 2002, there was an incident at an auto parts store (in Van Nuys, California) where a sales clerk was shot by a customer because the clerk wouldn't take back a set of (allegedly) faulty brake pads.

It's difficult to tell if the dog is only barking or if he is a serious biter. But these days, is it worth harassing the dog to find out?

CUSTOMERS JUST WANT YOU TO BE HONEST

The following letters aren't vicious or threatening. But they are sincere. Listen for the emotions they relay and the sense of helplessness.

The first example takes 'intimidation selling' to a new level.

This woman succumbed to the pressure of signing up for a health club membership. When she got home, her boyfriend was furious at how she was treated and demanded a refund. She hadn't even been a member for 12 hours (or used a single workout session) but the club refused to refund her money.

> *"I got a lot of pressure to sign the papers from the health club. I said I wanted to talk it over with my boyfriend and they said, "Well, I guess you aren't a good candidate for our club because you can't commit. People here are committed to fitness."*

This next woman just tried to rent a moving van.

> *"I tried to rent a van from Payless Car Rental in St. Louis, Missouri, in July 2003 (1) The operator didn't know the current location of the facility so I had to drive around and look for it. (2) They had no vans and sent me to Avis. I had to pay the difference (twice as much) and was promised a refund for the difference. (3) The refund was not only not processed on site after I turned the car in, it has never been processed. (4) Repeated phone calls and emails to the company have never been answered. The best answer I got (October 2003) was that the president of the company was "working on a personal letter" to all the people this has happened to. Well, it is almost February 2004—no letter— no refund—no response."*

> *Glenda E.*

This following complaint demonstrates how a lack of trust in one area can destroy loyalty for your other brands.

"I purchased a package of Irish Crème International creamers (single serving creamers) from the Dominicks Food Store in Morton Grove, Illinois. When I went to unpack my groceries I noticed that the expiration date on the package expired 4 months prior. I (went back to the store) told the lady at customer service that I would like to grab another pack that was not expired. But when I went back to get another pack, I noticed that ALL of them were expired. I tried another flavor and those were expired. I checked 6 boxes—all expired. The lady at the service desk was quite rude but gave me my money back; saying she would have all the expired boxes pulled from the shelf. I went back the next day and not only were the expired creamers NOT pulled, the box I returned was back on the shelf! I asked to speak to the manager. I was told he was not available but that he would call me. Never heard a word. A week later—still the expired products were on the shelf. The Customer Service Desk has an "I DON'T CARE" attitude. Every time I am there it appears the manager is in his little office joking around with other employees. I used to eat from their Salad Bar every day but after the creamer incident, I don't think I can trust them to keep fresh product in the store. Obviously they are not concerned for the health of their customers so I will not purchase from that location.

Sharon V.

Next is a thoughtful letter from a woman who thought she was taking the proper precaution.

"In February, we purchased a three piece sectional and an additional armless section from Robinson's May in Santa Ana, California. Along with the sectional, we purchased Miracle Seal Plus leather protection. When we submitted a claim, we were told the small tears were not sufficient damage. We spoke to a Miracle Seal rep in December and have not received a call back from a supervisor. I made another call to them this morning. I have re-faxed the receipts and am still waiting to hear. Meanwhile I have contacted Robinson's May—who sold me the warranty as a 5 year warranty against rips, tears, stains, lipstick stains, etc. They say it's not their problem; call Miracle Seal. Can someone out there please help me?

Wilma W.

Can you hear the desperation in her voice? Wilma was urged to buy an extended warranty in anticipation of something going wrong. Then when she tried to make a claim, she was told her damage wasn't large enough? I contacted Wilma to see if anyone ever followed up. She wrote back.

"The couch was never repaired by Robinson's May or Miracle Seal. After almost six months, Miracle Seal sent out a technician to "erase" the tears with a magic marker. Rudeness and poor customer service relations have become the norm and I myself feel we should not support

organizations that allow their employees to treat the consumer badly."

There is absolutely no excuse for rude behavior; especially on the telephone as new, prospective customers are trying to decide if they should spend money with you.

"I was letting my fingers do the walking in search of a Mother's Day gift and I saw an ad for the Bacchus and Venus Wine Shop in Sausalito, Calif. So, I called and the salesperson—and then manager were both extremely rude, the kind of hotshot attitude that sometimes follows wine snobs. The manager wouldn't even let me complete a sentence when I started asking questions. "Do you want to buy something or not, you're wasting my time", she said. I began to explain that I wanted to learn more before buying blind. And she sassed back at me with more attitude, and without a goodbye, she hung up on me. I immediately called back to hear her not-so-cheery voice. I said, "Did you hang up on me? Is that how you conduct business with your customers?" She said, "I have paying customers here in the store and you didn't want to buy, so I decided our conversation was over." And then she hung up again."

Peter W.

How about when the company tells you the problem is, *"in your imagination?"*

"I bought a counter depth GE Refrigerator approx. 1 1/2 years ago. The repairman was here 6 times before it was replaced. I am having the same

problems all over and GE refuses to address the problems. It doesn't get cold enough (I can't get a cold glass of milk even though I transfer my milk to glass bottles so that it will get colder). The freezer freezes everything except the ice cream; which never gets hard. I can dish it out with a spoon easily. I have the unit set at #9 (the maximum) and the repairman told me to keep milk in the very back where the cold comes out. I tried that and it doesn't help. I am wasting food. The first repairman said they made this model with the wrong type of fan. I don't want to throw the whole thing out. What are my options before eating the loss? It's still under warranty and they keep saying it's cold enough.

Gladys H. Oceanside, Ca.

We all have expectations of how a product or service should perform but her quote, "I can dish it out (ice cream) with a spoon" convinced us she had a valid complaint.

YOUR REACTION?

When you read these letters you probably had several reactions.

(1) "I've had a very similar experience and I empathize with these frustrations."

(2) "Why would a company hire such rude, uncaring people in the first place?"

(3) "Why are companies advertising one thing and delivering so short on their promise?"

(4) Don't they train people, these days?"

Well, I have my own question.

If customer service is dead, who or what was responsible for the murder?

WHAT KILLED CUSTOMER SERVICE?

CHAPTER 3

11 MAJOR SHIFTS IN OUR CULTURE

When I started doing some forensic pathology on the death of customer service, I came up with too many good suspects...starting with:

SHOPPING MALLS

The creation of the suburban shopping mall was one of the principal carriers of the disease that led to the eventual demise of common merchant courtesy and so-called "customer service." If that seems like a lot of blame to heap on a shiny, convenient building, read on.

In 1946, when Abraham Levitt developed Levittown (on Long Island) the first mass-produced low-cost housing tract was born.

The birth of the suburb.

Naturally, suburban home owners didn't want to trek into town for everyday goods and services. So, small "shopping centers" started to sprout.

By April of 1950, the Northgate "mall" opened just north of Seattle, Washington. Northgate provided 800,000 sq.

ft. of fully enclosed shopping—arranged in a linear pattern along a 44-foot wide pedestrian walkway called a "mall." That template would become the center spine of all future regional shopping centers.

Why was it called a mall? Legend has it the word stems from the British game of pall-mall, which combines elements of croquet and golf. Pall Mall has been played since the 1500's on a wide fairway green; much like the long, wide center corridor in any modern shopping mall.

I am old enough to remember life *before* malls. I grew up in a small town much like many small towns in America; McMinnville, Oregon—population 6,000. My dad was a crop dusting pilot/car salesman. My mom was a homemaker. My grandfather had the town's machine shop. And, my great uncle was the county "water witcher." Yes, he pointed sticks at the ground and found hidden well water. I don't know how he did it but he always found water and he never charged a dime for the service. Neighbors did those kinds of favors for each other in small towns.

We all went downtown to the J.C. Penney store for Christmas shopping. Woolworths was the obvious stop for "sundries"—which I later found out meant prescription medicines, sunglasses, and of course, Halloween costumes. We had a post office, a sewing store, a courthouse/jail, a feed store, a doctor's office, a lawyer or two, a Chinese restaurant, and every other necessary stand-alone purveyor of goods and services; happily ready to cater to all your daily needs. Oh, and if we didn't have what we needed in McMinnville, we could order it from the Montgomery Ward catalog.

Something lived within those storefront walls that were far more significant than the products they sold.

Accountability.

"Customer service" wasn't even a popularized phrase, yet. It wasn't something anyone really "practiced." Shopkeepers were friendly to their customers because they were neighbors. They liked each other. We would get our back-to-school clothes from Mrs. Simmons and then see her at the market...or show up at her house on Wednesdays for "game night." We'd get our health check-ups from Doc Hoffman; who not only cured our colds and fevers—but would rub our heads with his knuckles in church.

My gregarious father was the guy who usually organized the men's annual deer hunting trip. And, as was mandatory in those days, once a week he and his friends would get liquored up at the local Elks Club meeting.

Since we all knew each other, if a shop owner was unfriendly or ignored a "customer/neighbor" in any way, word got out faster than a cable modem. Chances are he or she would get a "talking to" from another neighbor and eventually visit the home of the offended party with an apology or a pie.

Shopping malls changed all that.

The shops and services that filled the malls were 2nd units of the downtown businesses. The owner might flit between locations but more often than not, he had to transfer an experienced downtown employee to the new location. Good for potential business but bad for the new employee; who was now displaced from *his* friends. No longer did he have to be held accountable to his neighbor. So, if a young clerk was frustrated with a customer, he or she could usually get away with being less than friendly. The clerk knew there was a remote possibility that he would ever run into that person in his home town. The lines of kindness, decency, and employment obligations were starting to blur. There was no one to answer to except the remote boss; who didn't live in the new neighborhood either.

Goodbye accountability.

CHAIN STORES

Chain stores hammered another nail in the customer service coffin.

When the mall caught on, more malls sprung up. Successful storeowners began to reserve space in any new location; hoping to make money on the economies of scale. That's why if you go to any medium to large sized mall (in any American city) you will see the same collection of stores. *Starbucks. Macy's. Ritz Cameras. Aunt Annies Pretzels. Hallmark. Wilson's Leather. Cinnabon. Victoria's Secret, Barnes & Noble*...you know the rest.

As you can probably guess, the managers of these chain stores are often recruited from the Mother Ship—or from other stores in the chain. These transplants typically have no personal connection to the community nor the vaguest idea of what makes the "locals" tick.

Do they care?

Well, they are "instructed" to care. But putting their hearts behind their work often takes a back seat to the quarterly sales goals that is tied to their compensation package.

It's easy to see how these managers can be detached on an emotional and financial level.

MERGERS & ACQUISITIONS

Mergers and Acquisitions haven't done any favors for customer service, either. Because technology made scalability viable in most every industry, buying a compatible company usually means instant revenue and greater productivity; with a smaller, integrated workforce. Unfortunately, the managers of these entities often confine their focus to "the numbers" assuming the human element will sort itself out.

We have seen these debacles in the H.R. training film business.

H.R. directors would shout. *"We're now twice as big as we were, overnight! Some of the folks are staying. Others are being laid off. Send us something to help get the survivors on the same page."*

We obeyed.

And, customer service got worse.

Why?

A structural change in any organization can't help but disrupt people. To make the merger happen, somebody had to cave in. And, as Tom Peters, told me, *"When an elephant swallows a mosquito, the mosquito will likely change first."*

Imagine two competing banks with two entirely different management styles. Imagine you are an employee who has come to believe in your bank's mission statement and you love your company culture. Your bank has worked hard to differentiate itself from the competition and you took pride in that accomplishment. There was camaraderie. Now, your competition has gobbled up your bank and expects you to join hands with the incumbent crew and happily assimilate.

You are expected to change religions; so to speak.

An arrangement like that breeds contempt and unrest. Trust must be rebuilt. And as a part of trusting the new management team, you want the new owners to appreciate your value in the organization.

During the inevitably awkward and fragile transition, even the most basic operations of billing and collecting money go through a series "fits and starts." Meanwhile, your newly combined customers stand helpless and frustrated; forced to eat the hors d'oeuvre they didn't order.

That's why a certain percentage of acquired customers jump ship.

I heard Chuck Burkett, President of *First Tennessee Bank*, tell his management team, *"We prefer to grow this company organically because you've all worked very hard to build our reputation and brand with our customers. And acquiring another bank usually results in a loss of 20% of the acquired customers."*

I attended a Hewlett Packard "management summit" shortly after their beleaguered merger with Compaq Computer. Talk about two bitter enemies being forced to live in the same apartment! There was so much tension in that room I should have been wearing a Kevlar vest. In a forum style "Q & A" session with some of the top brass, the employee questions were full of venom and animosity about who would be doing what job.

Do you think these folks had "customer care" at the top of their priority list?

Not on your life.

These displaced employees were more concerned with waging cubicle turf battles as the merger dust was settling.

THE "BIG BOX" PARADOX

Most of these retail behemoths have made the dreadful mistake that they can skimp on customer service if they offer incredibly low prices.

Not true.

Customers want low prices *and* good customer service.

We read a lot of complaint letters from people who shopped at what retail insiders refer to as the *Big Box* stores; those dynamo sized department stores like Wal*Mart, Best Buy, Office Depot, Home Depot, (and all other assorted depots).

SIDE NOTE: I had to exclude Costco Wholesale from the list because not a single complaint was recorded regarding this highly visible big box store.

As shocking as this may seem to you big box buyers, the customer doesn't care that your massive outlets have shed blood negotiating the best gross margins so you can offer that low, low price. And, they have no idea what hoops your wholesale suppliers have jumped through to get your business. Customers understand that you have "volume buying power" and that's why they can get a cheaper price on toothpaste and DVDs. But customers also want knowledgeable, caring, well informed, pleasant people to sell it to them. Just because you have been clever enough to offer a killer price doesn't give you an excuse to provide rude, incompetent service.

Customers want it all.

And if they don't get it all, they might commit the cardinal sin of buying elsewhere; at a higher price. Yes, your customers will pay more for decency, courteous behavior, and personal attention.

The problem is that big box management constantly pound "the profit margin process" into their managers—who, in turn, pound it into their employees—who likewise come to work with the overriding pressure that they must turn product.

That attitude can't help but permeate the transaction; leaving customers to feel like they are an inconvenience.

I had one assistant manager tell me, *"Most customers don't use their heads. They will hunt us down to ask us where the most obvious merchandise is...when it's right in front of their eyes. Why do you think we post those big signs?"*

These employees have an arrogance that subconsciously spits, *"We offer you the lowest prices and that should be enough. Can't you see I'm busy counting light bulbs right now?!"*

They have forgotten they are in the "solve problems" and "help people" business. Do-it-your-sellers go to *Home Depot* and *Lowe's* as much for the guidance and expertise as they do for the product.

On Saturday mornings, I've been at *Home Depot* to witness 3–6 year olds—with hammers and screwdrivers—taking classes on how to pound nails and screw screws. The object is to demystify a home improvement project and instill confidence in young people by making them feel successful. I suppose if the kids have a good experience they will become faithful Home Depot customers, as adults.

Nice plan.

But won't these new customers be surprised if they are ignored by the same people who taught them how to swing a hammer.

INTERNET COMMERCE IS AMAZING...BUT DEPERSONALIZING

In terms of getting the best price on anything from bubble wrap to a Shetland pony, the Internet has been the 8th wonder of the world. But in terms of promoting customer service, the Internet has caused way more harm than good.

Service, support, and accountability are now detached by half a world away. I dare say that, in your lifetime, you will never meet the person in a foreign country who helped you hook up your in-home wireless router. That is, if he or she actually helped you.

Forget the shopping mall.

Forget the downtown merchant.

Forget the glossy mail order catalog.

With a cheap computer and a dial-up connection, we can all buy and sell anything in the world—get the best price—and have it delivered to our front door; overnight.

And, we never even have to actually speak to anybody!

Global commerce does something else to customer service.

It nationalizes people—in a *bad* way.

We saw many complaints from people who were unable to understand the language on the other end of the call. Others had poor phone line connections and just gave up.

LANGUAGE BARRIERS ARE KILLING COMMERCE

The United States is not only the home of the free and the brave but the home of entrepreneurialism. Anyone with a good idea can come to the U.S.A. and make a fortune. The U.S. has experienced a global migration from Russia, the Middle East, China, Korea, Taiwan, and so many other countries because of that simple fact. However, the useful assimilation of the collective languages is lagging far behind. And, because anyone with an internet connection can buy and sell in the global economy, it's maddening to do business with people when they can't understand your language...and you can't understand theirs.

Edward C. Baig writes for USA Today and he penned a discouraging article titled: *Have you Tried to Get Tech Support Lately? Arrgh! #*!!*

> *"Many companies shave costs by placing call centers overseas, but the practice riles some*

customers. According to a survey published in the June Consumer Reports, 28% of people who phoned tech support seeking help with desktop PCs reported some kind of communication problem. More than six in 10 complained that the support staff's English was limited or very hard to understand."

My own mother, is a new computer user. She loves it for email and researching golf, gardening, and news stories. But when her computer went down, she was totally unable to understand the tech support people (there were many) who tried to reactivate her desktop. She can relate to Mr. Baig's next example.

"Retired and living near Birmingham, Ala., Dell customer James R. Barr, Sr. is neither geek nor novice. He uses the PC to surf, play games with the grandkids and pay bills.

Barr called Dell seeking help formatting, partitioning and reloading Windows XP. "I got a tech in India who spoke British English. I am 73, speak Alabama English and use two hearing aids. We both experienced some understanding problems."

It gets worse:

"One communications snag: The rep didn't realize that when Barr said "oh" he meant the number, not the letter. He (later) phoned Dell after the DVD player in his PC kept skipping. "The tech would ask me a question, leave to talk to someone else, ask me another question, leave to talk to another

person," Barr recalls. "(He) told me my service tag
(to identify my system) did not exist, insisted that
I reinstall XP and was generally not polite,
knowledgeable or interested in my problem."

Barr has had better luck with supervisors. "But
getting to them is like pulling hen's teeth. One
tech person indicated they didn't even have a
supervisor."

After (several) months, Barr's DVD player still
skips.

Baig found a woman who actually resented *herself* for trying
to make a point with a support person in another country.

"My issue is not that the help was offshore," says
Laurie Lago of Portland, Ore., a loyal Sony
customer until recently. "I resent that Sony
dumped service offshore without doing proper
training. The only way to break through is to
throw a tantrum and become an 'ugly American.'
I think I resent this most of all."

Sony's general manager of Vaio Service
Operations, Steven Nickel, says the company has
recently changed support partners who "weren't
meeting stringent requirements." And managers
who monitor live calls remotely from support
headquarters in Fort Myers, Fla., can now
intervene in a case as necessary, via instant
messages.

Mark Oldani, head of U.S. Consumer Tech Support
at Dell, concedes things aren't always perfect:
"We certainly understand on occasions we can

have hiccups like everyone else", he says. Dell ceased dispatching to India support calls from American corporate customers, amid complaints last fall. But many home users are routinely routed to a global call center. "Our expectation for performance is the same regardless of where a call is handled", Oldani says.

Oh, I'm sure tech folks get their share of first-time computer users who argue their "foot pedal" doesn't work...only to have a support person finally deduce they are talking about the mouse. But that's part of the job. Support people are paid to be patient, empathetic, and understandable.

Baig offers a solution.

"Preparing overseas staffers is not just about tweaking accents. It is about empathy training and beefing up cultural literacy. Microsoft asks foreign staffers to listen to National Public Radio broadcasts."

Hear that? Empathy training. Go back and underline those two words. You will need them later.

SOME COMPANIES GO "GLOBAL" TOO SOON

Companies who want to do business in the U.S.A. and/or other countries need to know that their "template" or "franchise model" might not smoothly dovetail into the local culture. These companies will fail miserably if they don't take into account the local customs, the tone and personality of the region, and the way commerce has been transacted for hundreds (maybe thousands) of years. Curt Coffman,

Gallup's Global Practice Leader—Customer and Employee Engagement; and author of *Follow This Path*. Curt wrote me to offer this insight:

> *"Organizations now have the challenge of creating a Global Brand Promise. What this has resulted in is a one-size-fits-all service strategy (largely driven by the U.S. and Europe)—and ignoring the local cultural tenets of doing business. This approach has been proven unsuccessful, as it tries to set forth the "7 Step Plan of Customer Service" to be implemented in ALL centers, stores or service outlets. The seven step approach not only minimizes the local customs, but sends the message that those customs are just wrong. Service varies by culture!*
>
> *What does transcend across cultures is the right "emotional outcomes" for each customer in each country. Confidence, Integrity, Pride, and Passion. Let these emotional outcomes transcend—not the "steps" and each culture will create these outcomes using local lore, approach and custom"*

THE MISGUIDED AMERICAN BACKLASH TO "OUTSOURCING"

I hear a lot of workers complain that customer service is suffering because so many jobs are being shipped overseas. They say they resent their companies for giving jobs to "foreigners" and that their attitude can't help but migrate to the customer.

So, should we assume that outsourcing is evil?

Nope. We've been sold a lie.

Outsourcing is the kind of inflammatory topic TV news directors salivate over. The media knows that the subject of outsourcing infuriates Americans because it means sending home grown jobs overseas. In fact, one study shows that 84% of Americans say it's bad for the economy.

That's not true. But if they believe it, it affects the public consciousness.

I used to believe outsourcing was dangerous, too.

As a college student, in the early 70's I worked part time as a longshoreman and Teamster in Seattle, Washington. So, I personally witnessed timber companies cut down trees and ship them to Asian countries for processing. Our foreman told us it was much cheaper to do that than mill them in our own home region. Pouring salt in that wound was seeing those logs redelivered to the Pacific Northwest to build gleaming new suburban homes. So, naturally I made the assumption that *all* outsourcing was bad for America.

I was categorically and statistically wrong.

I sat with Tom Donahue, the President of the *United States Chamber of Commerce*, just before he was about to speak to a group of insurance CEO's in Boca Raton, Florida. For obvious reasons, Tom is very interested in the outsourcing issue.

Over breakfast, Tom told me how he had been sensitive to the outcry and emotional damage done to small businesses in the U.S. over the outsourcing issue. His constituents wanted large companies to stop sending American jobs to Asia, India, and China. "Do something about it, Tom," was the message. Now, Tom is a guy who has the power to spend $30 million dollars on lobbying, every six months if he has to, to get the job done. If outsourcing was as dismal as he'd heard, he was going to kick, scream, and spend considerable cash to influence congress to get this travesty under control.

Tom Donahue is a formidable opponent to have against you.

I would guess Tom is in his 60's and a dead ringer for the late character actor, William Hickey, known to fans of *National Lampoon's Christmas Vacation*, as *Uncle Lewis*.

But to be clear, Tom doesn't wear a toupee. In fact, there is nothing phony about Tom.

I am also convinced that Tom expects to live another 180 years. He's fired up all the time. He's blunt. He's tough. Unafraid to offend.

When a man in the group approached him about not giving money to the John Edwards presidential campaign, Tom looked at him and said, *"You're not your mother's stupid son, are you? I'm not giving money to a guy who gets financed by the country's most egregious lawyers."*

That's Tom Donahue.

Before this job, he was the head of the American Trucking Association. So, he can be brilliantly political...or he can be a junkyard dog for his constituents.

However, the expensive report he commissioned shockingly demonstrated how wrong we all had been in our thinking. It turns out that outsourcing actually creates more jobs in the United States.

According to the report, *Jobs, Trade, Sourcing, and the Future of the American Worker*, *"The U.S. Chamber found little hard data to support fears about outsourcing and claims of an impending exodus of U.S. jobs overseas."* Beyond that, the Chamber report noted that we should be celebrating the vast creation of jobs in the U.S. by foreign firms who have investments and operations in our country. Tom was emphatic when he said, *"Our report shows that foreign business creates far more jobs in the United States than are lost to overseas markets."* To be specific, the report discovered that, *"direct foreign investment now exceeds $487 billion and supports 64 million jobs in the United States. In fact, looking at services trade, in-sourcing beats outsourcing by early $60 billion annually. The McKinsey Global institute even estimates that every dollar of cost the United States moved offshore brings America a net benefit of $1.12 to $1.14."*

Today, Tom leads the charge to stop proposed legislation that would impede American companies from doing reciprocal business overseas. Tom pulls no punches when he says, *"Building a wall around this country by limiting business options is a failed economic model and a violation of our own trade agreements, which could start a trade war."*

He's not alone.

Former DHL Chairman, Uwe Doerken, is also a huge champion of outsourcing. As you know, DHL is in the worldwide package delivery business. Doerken told USA Today, *"It's a mistake to tax companies to stop offshoring. First of all offshoring benefits the consumer. More efficient and less costly production leads to more affordable products and services and allows companies in higher-labor-cost economies like the USA and Europe to stay competitive and preserve their remaining jobs."*

It's funny that we can sit around the Plasma TV and delight in the fact that consumer electronics are getting cheaper, yet we forget how that actually happens.

Again, because we hear so much about off shoring jobs, enough people start to believe it. And that does affect the national customer service attitude. In this case, let's be brave and *not* let the rumor become the truth.

THE 'CUSTOMER ORIENTED' WORK FORCE IS BAILING OUT

Customer service is going to get really bad in the next 10 years because we are running out of "old school" workers.

According to the Bureau of Labor Statistics of the U.S. Department of Labor (sounds like a really fun group) "Over the next 30 years, 60 million Americans will retire. By 2010, America will have 168 million jobs and only 158 million Americans in those jobs."

See what I mean? We're going to have 10 million more jobs than we have workers to fill them. I had the opportunity to meet Alexis Herman, the brilliant former Secretary of Labor during the Clinton administration, and I asked her if she thought those numbers were accurate. Herman told me, *"I think those figures are on the low side. The number of jobs to fill may go much higher. We have not yet begun to feel the burden of not having enough workers in this country. And, most of those jobs would benefit the lower income households."*

If baby boomers are reaching retirement age, and younger generations are waiting longer to have children, where will we find the workers?

(The weak of heart may leave the room.)

The workforce vacuum can only be filled if we change immigration laws so that we can hire foreign workers.

Don't even pretend to be surprised.

Already, it is estimated there may be as many 10 million undocumented workers in the U.S. doing work we take for granted; construction, landscaping, health care, agriculture, restaurants, hotels, and well...anything else we refuse to do. If employers complain that they can't find good help now, what are they going to do when there is nobody to hire?

What will happen to customer service, then?

That's why businesses hire futurists and demographic consultants. So they can verify this startling data and hopefully shine some light on a solution.

I get to hear a lot of those types on the lecture circuit. Most of them are tedious and boring.

I finally met one who wasn't.

I was standing in the wings—waiting to go onstage—and I asked the PowerPoint operator, "Who is that chain smoking, uncomfortably hunched man, huddling in the corner?" He said, "That's Dick Hokenson, the demographer."

What Dick Hokenson lacked in off-stage presence was overshadowed by his brilliantly dry sense of humor in talking about his passion; demographics of the current and future workforce. Dick said, *"In this country we are open to immigration; especially illegal immigration."* He took another shot by saying, *"I have five children because I know the truth about social security."* Then, he turned serious. *"The birthrates have dropped and baby boomers are not generating replacements for themselves anymore. We know our workforce is going to disappear so we are looking offshore for workers. But China is aging faster than anyone and will run out of workers in 20 years. Why? Because there aren't enough men left over there. You want men, go to Alaska where the odds are good…but then again, the goods are odd."*

Pretty funny, right?

Dick said he is distressed by what is happening in Europe. "Business is so bad and the workforce is so sparse that shop keepers aren't even restocking the shelves. I went to buy a DVD player and all they had were floor models," he said. Dick also agrees that the only way to replace workers is to change immigration laws. Dick is suggesting we adopt an almost global migration mentality when he says, *"Let workers flock to the business centers and to the companies who are producing; like farm workers who invade the San Joaquin Valley during harvest season."*

If we don't, there may be no one available to deliver even a modicum of customer service.

SOME ORGANIZATIONS FEEL PRESSURE TO LOWER EMPLOYMENT STANDARDS

If we are running out of workers and we won't open the borders, some employers are starting to think of lowering employment standards as an option. And, for the rest of you who complain, *"Aw c'mon, I'm always hearing we have so many Americans out of work. How about putting some of those homeless people and welfare recipients to work? Why can't we train them and give them jobs?"*

We're trying!

I was in Birmingham, Alabama speaking to the *Central Alabama Workforce Department* and I met their brilliant Birmingham Commissioner. Her name is Sheila Smoot and she told the audience something that stunned us all. Sheila related a recent conversation she'd had with the manager of a new Mercedes Benz assembly plant recently built in Alabama. *"The HR director from Mercedes Benz factory said he can't find workers. We have 500 jobs and we can't fill them with Alabamans because they cannot pass the drug test."* It used be we'd ask, *"Where are the jobs in Alabama? Well, we have the jobs. Now we're asking you, where are the workers?"*

How can this be?

The employment/unemployment cycle they are trying to break in Alabama is that there are too many 3rd generation welfare recipients; who find it much easier to follow the path of their parents (and grandparents) than take the time and effort to get an education and a job.

This isn't just happening in Alabama.

Shift4 is a very successful credit card data software company in Las Vegas, Nevada. In fact, when you zip your credit card through a machine and get an instant approval, you are probably using their software. The owner and his wife told me, *"20% of the people who apply with us cannot pass the drug test or the background checks. It's tough finding enough good people; even in a rapidly growing population town like Las Vegas."*

Still think lowering the employment standards is a good idea? Are you sure you want customer service from a compromised workforce?

CHAPTER 4

CUSTOMERS BLAME THE YOUNGER WORKFORCE

We read countless letters from customers and managers who complained that, *"Young people just don't understand basic courtesies or a good work ethic."* They characterized "younger" as "the under 30 crowd."

If young people are the torchbearers of our future, then why are so many customers and employers pulling their hair out over this highly educated, seemingly "emotionally detached" younger workforce? Well, even though they have been raised and schooled by baby boomers, they don't think or act like boomers. They are not motivated by the same incentives. Hence, they cannot be trained like boomers. They have their own sense of values and emotionality. It's our job to know what drives them. We must adapt our training in ways that motivate them to behave within your company culture so that everyone gets what they want.

But first, let's examine who your customers are talking about and how they think.

YOUNG WORKERS JUMP JOBS TOO QUICKLY

Lev Grossman wrote in *Time* magazine about a young woman named Ellen who's had seventeen jobs since 1996. In fact, the Grossman article targeted young people 24–28 years old and found that many had a hard time keeping the same apartment for very long. Many wanted (and succeeded) in moving back home when they decided to jump jobs.

Why are they so fickle?

Grossman wrote,

> *"They like to dress and talk and party like they did in their teens. They date a lot, can't keep a mate for very long, and were all about having fun. They are not interested in settling down. They don't want responsibilities, at least for now. The irony is that these people do want to prepare for adulthood. In fact, they say they don't want to make a mistake about their career path so they are taking their time."*

American social scientists are calling these people TWIXTERS. They are stuck between adolescence and adulthood. In England the same group is called KIPPERS; which stands for, *"kids in parents pockets eroding retirement savings."* As youngsters, we parents regularly congratulated them on every tiny success. We coddled these kids. I remember a teacher telling me that building our child's self esteem was the most important gift we could bestow. So, we gave them mock trophies and special privileges *not* for finishing in first, second, or third place...but for simply participating in an activity. Dustin Hoffman, playing Ben Stiller's father in the movie *Meet the Fockers* proudly shows off his son's 9th place ribbons. The baby boomer audience members howled because we've all done that. We drove our kids to their soccer camps, interpretive dance lessons, karate classes, ski schools, and sent them off to great universities. Then, we cried with joy as they walked down the aisle with a prestigious sheepskin.

We cried again when they moved back home.

What went wrong?!

We thought we raised our children to be responsible, productive adults. But once these kids were faced with actually finding work and starting a truly independent life, they discovered they were college graduates who lacked real world skills. Some are perturbed that they have to start at the bottom and work their way up. To add insult to injury, they have monstrous school loans strapped to their backs. A *Time* survey showed that 66% owe more than $10,000. Five percent owe more than $100,000.

You better believe that money is a huge concern for these kids. They would like to be totally independent but their salaries don't make ends meet.

Most parents I know are still contributing a few thousand dollars a year to help subsidize high apartment costs, cell phone bills, car and health insurance.

Chances are some of these young people are working for you; until they get bored.

And, that should worry you.

We heard complaints that younger workers displayed more open contempt for the workplace (and their manager) than older workers. Clerks would roll their eyes at management in front of the customer. They didn't think it was wrong to use profanity in front of a customer. And, (unsolicited) would say things to the customer like, *"I don't blame you for being mad, dude. This place sucks and the manager is an idiot."*

An HR director for a leading national department store chain told me,

> *"When I started in HR twenty years ago, we wouldn't even consider hiring a person whose previous job only lasted a year. Today, it's common to see previous jobs that only lasted a few months. It's harder and harder to keep these young employees because they're so fickle. They'll leave if they don't get enough training or perks. What's even more insulting is that the training they want is something they plan to use for their next job. They seem to jump at the first sign of a better offer. They are all about 'what's in it for me'. They have seen their parents lose their jobs in a merger or an acquisition and have to relocate the family. So they think of loyalty as a myth."*

I asked her how her company handles this problem.

> *"We would never admit this publicly but our attitude is if they are using us, then we are going to get as much out of them as long as we have them around. Some burn out. But we still have to make a profit."*

Employers think these young workers leave because the wages aren't high enough. If that is the case, how much money do they need and what are they spending it on?

Catherine Stellen is the Vice President of Marketing & Trends at *Youth Intelligence*. *Youth Intelligence* is a research firm who studies how this demographic spends money. She told a small group of us,

"We asked them if we gave them $500 would they spend it on a product or an experience. They overwhelmingly said 'experience.' They want to say they have done something cool. They also use their money to join clubs for the experience of meeting other people. Poker clubs are popular. They go to cooking classes, shooting clubs, and movieoke."

Canon Inc., Vice President, Elliot Peck, told me he believes that's why digital photography is so popular. *"The cameras are small so they can take them everywhere they go and record their experiences. Then, they can instantly relive the experience or share it with all of their friends over the Internet or on their cell phones."*

Beyond the "experience"—for these young people, the "better offer" isn't always about money. They are leapfrogging from company to company—or city to city—in a quest for the job they will love doing, every day. They don't even care if changing jobs is a move up. Also, the company brand name, size, and reputation isn't as important as the *feeling* they get from doing the work. They want to do something worthwhile and be able to capitalize on their talents. They want to matter in the world. According to Stellin, the reason they want to document their lives on personal websites, get involved in scrapbooking, and hold book club meetings—is so they can discuss things like relevance, relationships, and how they fit into the "big picture."

CONTRARY TO WHAT YOU MIGHT THINK, THEY DON'T ALL HAVE A.D.H.D.

I've heard employers complain that young workers can't stay focused. This is a serious issue because focus is required for any kind of effective business execution and pro-ductivity.

So why can't they focus? With movies, TV, and video games moving much more quickly (visually) than they did twenty years ago, you would think their finely tuned senses could grasp and process more information than workers from two decades ago.

Wrong.

TV producers say the heightened pace is in response to holding a young mind's, easily distracted, attention span. In TV production meetings I've heard producers say, *"We need an MTV producer for this project. It needs to have lots of pace!"* A three minute music video can sometimes contain over 600 "quick cut" scene changes. Bill Nye (aka The Science Guy®) once told me that, for his children's science show, his goal was to have a different camera move, a different scene, or a new sound effect every eight seconds—in order to hold the audience's (8–14 year olds) attention. These days, movie cameras shift up, down, upside down, and sideways so often that some people have reported leaving the theater with nausea and motion sickness.

And have you noticed how many younger people seem to have been "diagnosed" with ADHD (Attention Deficit Hyperactivity Disorder) and other attention disorders? Did an attention deficit epidemic suddenly mutate? Did "quick cut" media cause the problem? Some child rearing experts blame our society for over-stimulating our youth. After all, people have 300+ television channels to choose from. If they look for a job on Monster.com they'll have to decide between 750,000 choices. How about dating? Currently, online dating services list more than 15 million potential mates from which to choose. And, they date *those people* faster than ever before.

Have you heard about Speed Dating?

For you single people on the prowl, here's how it works.

A group of 10 or 12 men and women meet at a neutral location. A moderator randomly "pairs up" couples to talk. When the moderator starts the clock, the couples have two minutes to get to know each other. When the time is up, they move on to a new person. This musical chair process goes on until everyone has cycled through.

The organizers say that most people waste too much time and money on bad dates. They argue that you can know, within two minutes, if there is a "connection" worth pursuing. That means they are judging potential mates in micro-time. Is that fair? Is *short term attraction* a reliable window into a person's character? Is it respectful? Is it indicative of good decision making?

Whatever their rationale for compressing life's timing, the volume of input and distractions are real. Even college students recognize they can't stay focused on their school-work. Many will go to great lengths to secure a dose of the ADHD drug, Ritalin. They pop a pill in preparation for exams. Linda Ciampa, a CNN correspondent, reported on this phenomenon back in 2001.

> "...across college campuses, some students are taking Ritalin without a prescription, illegally, and they're using it to fuel everything from all-night study sessions to all-night parties. Last summer, a survey at the University of Wisconsin found that 20 percent of college students had taken Ritalin without a prescription."

That's a pretty startling number when it is largely considered that only 3–7% of all people are accurately diagnosed with ADHD.

So, if our young people can't stay focused long enough to take a test, how can they stay focused long enough to create and sustain a career?

And, if they can't stay loyal to their jobs or their mates, how can we expect them to reinforce loyalty to the customers they serve?

MAYBE WE SHOULD BLAME THE PARENTS?

Let's assume some of us haven't raised our children very well.

Sometime in the communal early 70's, on the extreme west and east coasts, we stopped teaching our children to refer to our adult friends as Mr. and Mrs. In an effort to treat our children as our friends, we blurred a line of respect for our children's elders. However, in the midwest and southern states I still hear children, of all ages, respond to their elders with, "Yes, sir." And, "No thank you, Ma'am." That simple hierarchical delineation, between adults and young people, was dropped in order to make a "closer connection" to the younger generation. So when our kids entered the workplace, that omitted component occasionally turned to blatant disrespect. Sometimes it bordered on contempt.

Contempt is a bad attribute for serving anybody.

Furthermore, the baby boomer generation almost made divorce a hobby. While the divorce rate of 50% isn't accurate, (Harris polls calculate it is more like 22%) divorce is still too easy for couples to accomplish. According to wedding researcher, Jeanne Hinds,

"The reason why combined divorce statistics have risen over the years is due to the advent of

no-fault divorces. Marriages had a tendency of staying together when alimony was more of a reality but with no-fault divorces, divorce became much easier to acquire and many people have exited long-standing marriages."

Children of divorced couples become embarrassingly spoiled. If there is a remarriage, the kids inherit a double set of grandparents (and a quantum set of new relatives). The kids also acquire more birthday presents than any child has the ability to count. I will never forget when my son, Ryan, turned 6 years old. He sat before an ocean of presents; which barely receded with the dipping horizon. He waded in; shredding through the wrappings, quickly glancing at the remote control car, the professional Lego collection, the motorized skateboard, or whatever it was—without even acknowledging the gift givers.

I was horrified and embarrassed.

I stopped him and said, "Ryan, slow down and say thank you." Because he was so overwhelmed with the sheer volume of presents, he didn't think he was doing anything wrong. In his little mind, he was just being efficient.

As a coping mechanism, psychologists tell us that divorce causes children to become physically and morally desensitized. If they are constantly shuttled between homes, they find ways to battle the insecurity of how (and where) they fit into the world. Some kids think the divorce was caused by something *they* did. Others retreat to their bedrooms and learn to compartmentalize their feelings; depending on which parent they're with at the time. And, when the children can't "deal," some parents medicate them with assorted anti-depressants—or take them to any number of recommended child shrinks to work out their anger and frustration. Psychologists wail pearls like, "Your feelings are real"—"Own your feelings"—"You have a right to feel this way." Consequently children quickly learn to play on their parent's guilt and attempt to get away with screaming, shouting, and violently disrespectful behavior. After all, children now have a license-to-misbehave because the family problems are *not their fault.*

But let's be honest, bad behavior *is* the child's fault and dismissing bad behavior discounts "owning" any accountability. Why would that mixed message *not* find its way into the workplace?

Want further examples of the desensitization of this emerging workforce?

Video games, which started out as *Pong,* evolved into *Grand Theft Auto; San Andreas.* If you are not familiar with the latter, players are encouraged to develop relationships with hookers, thieves and gangsters in order to score. Sure, people get killed along the way, but how else can you win, right?

OR, MAYBE WE SHOULD BLAME THE TEACHERS!?

Hold on! Aren't we in the middle of the glory days of the *No Child Left Behind* program? Aren't kids supposed to leave school better equipped for the job market? If that's the case, why are so many companies still lamenting that they don't have enough educated, qualified people to choose from?

The teachers I've talked to say, *"The 'No Child Left Behind' program simply doesn't work."*

The program was designed to emphasize standardized testing scores. It was supposed to ensure that all students got a fair and balanced education; regardless of socioeconomic conditions. Then, every May, students take these important standardized tests so that school districts can measure their success against others. The ranking is important for each school's collection of state funding.

High scores are good.

Low scores are bad.

Repeatedly low scores mean the school goes on probation—or worse. At this writing, in San Bernardino County, California alone, 17 schools are "on probation" for low scores. In the state of California, if a school has a low test score—and they don't raise that score, the state has the right to come in and take over. This prospect terrifies teachers...but it shouldn't.

Seriously, what will the state do? Take over with what? With whom? Do teachers really believe there is a ready surplus of qualified personnel to commandeer 17 schools? California doesn't even have enough certified teachers to fill the current jobs!

Anyway, you can imagine the constant pressure on school administrators (and teachers) to perform.

Here is how the student (and our future workforce) suffers.

At the beginning of the year, a teacher gets his/her classroom allotment of students. However, only the students who *started* the school year "count" in the eventual testing.

Yes, you read that correctly.

If a new student transfers into the classroom, mid-year, that student isn't counted in the standardized test score. Well, if you are a student who doesn't matter to the cumulative test score, you are bound to get neglected by the teacher. After all, the teacher is also judged by the test scores and will gravitate toward focusing on the remaining "counted" students. One teacher reluctantly admitted, *"I know it's sad—but the mid-year transfers don't get the extra tutoring time or my attention because I have my hands full worrying about the kids whose test scores matter."*

Furthermore, the volume of mandatory teaching material is so vast teachers find themselves racing through the material without time for discussion. One 5th grade teacher told me, *"It just occurred to me that (because of the volume of prescribed material) I can't remember the last time we've had an in depth class discussion about the subject. In the old days, kids asked questions and learning critical thinking was almost natural. These kids have no idea how to ask questions because we simply don't have time for that."*

How can a student be prepared to enter the workforce if they lack critical thinking and discussion skills?

These children are doomed to repeated job failures if they don't know how to ask questions, express a thought, or collaborate with their co-workers.

I spoke to an HR executive at the Nordstrom Department stores and he said he could fill an afternoon with horror stories about trying to get an applicant to communicate. *"These kids don't know how to talk to people. How can I put them on the telephone or on the sales floor if they don't have any communication skills?"*

ARE YOUNG WORKERS TOO NUMB TO LEARN HUMANITY?

Like a lot of people, I have been appalled at how young people inhumanely treat each other. I've even wondered if movies (which are so graphically realistic) and their depiction of violence have numbed their collective psyche?

With the technological advances in film making, great directors can create movies that look more authentic than ever before. With incredible digital clarity and 7.1 surround sound, we can be transported into the bloody boots of a soldier fighting for his life at Omaha Beach (*Saving Private Ryan.*)

To test my theory, I was curious if real life warriors (of this younger generation) made any correlation between actual combat and the video games they played or movies they watched as kids.

I only had to go to www.asoldiersblog.com.

You can hear from these short bursts of soldier comments how one leader eventually compares his missions with movie scenes.

> *The leader is Lt. Nathan Fick, commander of Bravo Second Platoon. He and his platoon are penetrating central Iraq sometime in 2003.*
>
> *Fick holds a briefing for his platoon's team leaders. "The bad news is, we won't get much sleep tonight," he says. "The good news is, we get to kill people."*
>
> *Fick jumps out of his vehicle and runs into the center of the melee in order to direct the Humvees, still jammed up in the kill zone, to safety. With his 9 mm pistol raised in one hand, Fick almost appears to be dancing on the pavement as streams of enemy machine-gun fire skip past his feet. He later says he felt like he was in a shootout from The Matrix.*
>
> *Fick is less than cheerful about the prospect of driving into Al Hayy—First Recon now has fewer than 300 Marines going into a city of 40,000.*
>
> *After briefing his men, he (Fick) says privately to me, "This is Black Hawk Down sh** we are doing."*

Is the comparison of a real battle to a movie battle desensitizing, fantasizing, or just a coping mechanism to survive an unspeakable situation? Actually, it doesn't matter which explanation you buy into, the result is the same. The intensity and "reality" of today's movie experience can make the *real thing* nearly pale by comparison.

When I first saw the pictures (on broadcast TV) of the prisoner abuse from the Abu Ghraib prison, in Iraq, I was sickened. The initial excuse for these shocking photos was sold as, "softening prisoners for questioning." Look, I know that interrogation, for the purpose of gathering "intelligence" isn't supposed to be pretty. I endorse doing whatever soldiers need to do to get life saving, war-shortening "Intel." But c'mon, these prisoners were being sexually humiliated for sport, not intelligence. What kind of American poses, smiling, behind a pyramid of naked prisoners?

Would you hire *that* guy to negotiate with your customers?

Do movie confrontations, between the hero and villain, explain why your younger employees might "explode" at a customer during a routine conflict?

OLDER CUSTOMERS WANT YOUNG WORKERS TO RESPECT THEIR BUYING POWER

A common complain from baby boomer customers was this: "Younger workers ignore me. They act like I'm insignificant. If they only knew how much money I have to spend."

Perhaps the most discouraging (and inaccurate) assumption made by younger workers is that older people aren't valued buyers.

Last year, I was asked to be the keynote speaker for a mid-level retail chain of clothing stores. The 25-ish Vice President, who spoke before me, actually said, *"You are our finest young lions. Don't spend so much of your energy with the older shoppers. They can waste your time with their endless stories. Remember, we are all about serving the youth culture, not ancient history."*

When it was my turn to talk, I offered to return my speaking fee if I was allowed to dispute him. I did dispute him—and they didn't want to return my fee.

The truth is this: You should *never* underestimate the buying power of your older customers!

Having a person over 55 ask if you for a "senior citizen discount" shouldn't lull you into thinking they are scraping by on a meager fixed income. All evidence shows that your older customers have a lot of extra money to spend. Furthermore, with the advances in healthcare, these people are going to be around for a long time to spend it.

At a tech event in Florida, that focused on the so-called "Youth Market," I met Maddy Dychtwald, author of *Cycles; How We Live, Work, and Play*. Maddy is a great champion of the baby boomer generation and beyond. She described how her mother had recently gotten remarried (in her 70's) and was looking forward to a long and happy marriage. As a daughter, Maddy admitted the ensuing nuptials were a bit unsettling for her. But, as a researcher, Maddy appreciated that her mom was proof positive that her work was spot-on target.

> *"Women are living 8–10 years longer than men and they are buying everything. Remember, the national institute on aging says that by 2050 the life expectancy will be 90–95 years old. In fact, long term investments means something very different when you look at it like that. It's*

no wonder that health care is the fastest growing industry because of this. Older customers have lots of money to spend and lots of time to spend it."

According to David Wolfe and Robert Snyder who wrote the book *Ageless Marketing*, The statistics show that 44–65 is the hottest new market. It is, *"45% larger than 18–43 and will be 60% larger by 2010."* As they write in their book,

"44–65 is the new consumer majority. "The New Consumer Majority is the only adult market with realistic prospects for significant sales growth in dozens of product lines for thousands of companies."

Want proof that baby boomers spend a lot of money?

These days, 60 year old accountants are convinced they can be Tina Turner, Mick Jagger, David Bowie, and Paul McCartney!

For the past two years, I have been fortunate enough to be the keynote speaker for NAMM (National Association of Music Merchants). NAMM is an enormous event that draws thousands of musicians, music store owners, celebrities (and wannabe players like me) to see the latest and greatest musical instruments and recording equipment. I have seen 55+ men and women happily lay out four thousand dollars for a new *Taylor* acoustic guitar—or six thousand dollars on a new digital "home" recording studio. These "older" people have lots of discretionary income—and are spending it on high end items they couldn't afford when they wanted to start a rock band at 17.

I did a program for the AARP and found they were passionate about providing opportunities for their energetic, active members who are 65, retired, bored, and starting a new career.

Second and third careers are getting quite common now.

Men and women who have worked until retirement, (in a job they didn't love), are finding new energy and purpose in finally being able to pursue something they truly want to do. I mean, if we are all going to live until we are 95, what are you going to do with the last 30 years of your life? Sit around? Or, will you create a brand new "retirement plan?"

That is surely the case of Isaac, a 68 year old man I met in Reno, Nevada. Isaac has worked his entire life as a postal carrier but his true love is gardening. He told me he subscribes to six horticultural magazines so that he can stay abreast of all the latest growth chemicals and soil combinations.

Incidentally, I do not.

As you can imagine, he can talk about vegetables for hours. When Isaac retires, next year, he and his wife are planning to move to Tucson, Arizona and raise super-sized tomatoes and sell them to the area restaurants.

Because Isaac has a natural interest and passion for the subject, I have no doubt he will become the tomato king of Arizona. If so, he is bound to accumulate a lot of extra money in *his* 2nd 401-K plan.

SO, HOW DO WE ENCOURAGE & MOTIVATE THE YOUNGER WORKFORCE TO EXECUTE PROFITABILTY?

If the experienced workforce is retiring and the younger workforce is unfocused, desensitized, and fickle, how do we bridge the gap and stay profitable? You do it by understanding that today's workforce thinks and acts differently than the "boomers." You'll stay competitive and attract the best talent by changing your 'employee care and feeding' habits. It's a different game out there and denial won't help you through it. One great example is coming up in the chapter titled, *Know Your Employees Hidden Desires.* Pay particular attention to the section; *The Best Incentive System I've Ever Seen.*

We are so committed to advancing the empathy approach to attracting, motivating and keeping good young people that we have formed a new business unit called:

The Customer Empathy Institute ™

The Customer Empathy Institute™ focuses on the systemic motivation and training of internal and external customer empathy. We work in tandem with an organization's behavior based customer-centric culture to prove how this single attitudinal element can exponentially increase profits and employee retention. The program will soon include open enrollment classes that will qualify as continuing education credits. There will be highly trained faculty members who will do on-site training and remote training; at the organization's location.

As you'll see by the examples in this book, implementing customer empathy is the next great profit generating engine.

10 BIG CHANGES YOU NEED TO MAKE IF YOU WANT THEIR LIFETIME LOYALTY!

CHAPTER 5

BIG CHANGE #1
DON'T LIE TO...OR
CHEAT YOUR
CUSTOMERS

No accusations, here. Our research showed that only a tiny percentage of customers paid for something they didn't receive. So, I realize you don't knowingly lie or cheat your customers. But, every time you don't deliver on your promises your customers will *feel* cheated and lied to. Remember, 34% of the customer complaints said they felt lied to and cheated when the organization didn't give them what they expected. When the customer was promised something (in person, in your advertising, store signage, or over the phone) and you failed to deliver, they not only felt suckered into the purchase, they felt stupid and "beat themselves up" for making such a bad choice.

No business was ever built on a foundation of customers who felt cheated.

THE ADVERTISING PROMISE DOESN'T TRICKLE DOWN

Advertising and marketing departments often work in vain because their carefully crafted messages can be so easily overshadowed by management's sales focus.

Organizations spends thousands...sometimes millions of dollars to attract potential customers and create leads for the company. The creative men and women in the Ad group painstakingly research target markets, prime demographics, and competitive advantages. Then, they stay up late—for months—designing colors, logos, tastes, sex appeal, jingles, and hiring celebrity spokespeople to get that targeted customer through the front door. To be successful, they need to appeal to as many of the customer's *emotional triggers* as they can. Their goal is, "To get into the customer's heart." Tugging at a customer's emotions is what moves consumers to act—to think about spending their money. Still, the best the Ad department can hope for is to create leads.

So, let's say the Ad department has accomplished their objective.

It is the responsibility of the rest of the company to follow through on the *emotional promise* made by the media message. If the company delivers everything the customer expects, the company will have their first shot at developing a return customer.

If the company fails to deliver on that "advertised promise" (as our research showed) the customer will feel lied to and cheated.

Because I go to a lot of sales meetings, I am often privy to the "roll out" of the company's newest media campaign—the coming "attractions" so to speak. It's a highly anticipated part of any meeting.

In fact, it's staged like a show!

To make the biggest impression on the sales force, the new commercials are usually broadcast on several 30 foot wide movie screens. Predictably, there is always a thunderous roar of applause afterward because the sales team now has proof that the company is spending big dough to support the sales effort.

I spoke at a large convention for Canon cameras where Canon's ad agency showed off their newest TV commercials.

The ads were heartwarming and overflowing with laughing children and loving parents. The commercials were accessible to a wide range of customers; giving them several emotional reasons to own these wonderfully simple-to-operate cameras. And, of course, there was a demonstration of the latest "bells and whistles" to assuage the techies.

As a consumer, I was sold.

I, myself, was looking to buy a video camera and was totally convinced that I could capture the precious, fleeting moments of our family's life with the most dependable instrument on the market.

When the room lights came back on, the sales manager got on stage to deliver his, "Where do we go from here?" speech.

That's when all of the emotion dropped dead.

He talked about the camera's price and the competition's market share. He brought up last year's numbers and next year's target. But not once did he reinforce the powerful emotional components we'd just witnessed on that giant TV screen. If he could have fired up his team with what these cameras will mean to the people who eventually buy them, the sales force could have gone back to their customers with a "story." A good story is the arousing ammunition necessary to provide the customer with an emotional connection that would produce ongoing profits. But that wasn't the story this manager had in mind. He was all about the numbers.

Fast forward one month.

I take a drive to *Fry's Electronics* in Huntington Beach, California to buy one of the fabulous video cameras I'd seen at the Canon convention. When I got to the video department, I picked up the camera, turned it on, and tried to remember some of its amazing "effects" features. The clerk saw me struggling but refused to look up from the latest issue of *Stuff* magazine. Finally, I said, "Excuse me, can you tell me how to activate some of these video effects?" He begrudgingly put down his magazine, came over (without saying a word) and took the camera out of my hands. "I'm not sure but I think it's this button," he grunts.

Then, he walked away!

So did I.

I went to a nearby *Best Buy* store where I met a slightly more knowledgeable teen-sales-clerk who found the manual and we both discovered how to use the features. I badly wanted the camera so I made a mercy purchase from this kid because, at least, he tried.

But, I blame his manager and my friends at Canon for not consistently training the emotional promise they made in their advertising. I had personally witnessed that beautiful message get totally discarded at the big sales rally. The advertising department had teed up the ball and nobody made an effort to keep swinging at it.

SELL THE EMOTIONAL STORY

Hitting sales targets are important. But the customer doesn't want to do business with human *transaction machines*. They want to spend money with enthusiastic ambassadors. And our "ambassadors" can't be our champions if we don't instruct them how (and when) to tell "the emotional story" behind our goods and services.

CHAPTER 6

BIG CHANGE #2
KNOW YOUR
EMPLOYEES
HIDDEN DESIRES

Forget about your leading edge product delivery technology and your "Customer Relations Management" software tools for just a moment. Our research overwhelming told us:

> YOU CAN'T HAVE A STRONG CUSTOMER SERVICE CULTURE UNLESS YOUR EMPLOYEES LOVE WHAT THEY DO

So, how do you do that?

You have to know what motivates your people from the inside out.

If you're a leader, you've got to get inside your people like an MRI machine. Find out what passions your people naturally possess. Learn what hobbies they favor, the magazines and books they read, and what sites they surf on the Internet. Find out what excites them. Then, honor them enough to put them in jobs that will help them succeed.

Stephen Covey writes in *The 8th Habit*,

> *"The team must have a spirit of mutual respect so that the strengths of each are acknowledged and utilized, and the weaknesses are made irrelevant by the strengths of the others."*

EXPLOIT YOUR CO-WORKERS...*FOR EVERYONE'S BENEFIT*

I didn't "get it" when it came to exploiting people's hidden desires until I met William Nye.

Bill Nye...aka...Bill Nye the Science Guy® is a man with enormous hidden desires and strengths—and he almost never got to use them.

Bill is one of my oldest and dearest friends. He is a Cornell graduate who studied under Carl Sagan. He knows more than you or I ever will know about earth, sea, and space science. It's easy for him to be excited about science stuff because science (and science education) are his passions. They are his purpose. Today, Bill commands huge speaking fees all over the world to talk about those subjects. Surprisingly, Bill would tell you he never would have thought of the "Science Guy" idea on his own.

Shockingly, I did.

Yes, *I* was the guy who came up with the idea to call Bill Nye "The Science Guy!"

When I first met Bill, he was winning Steve Martin look-a-like comedy contests. He loved performing comedy and would have done anything to quit his full time aerospace engineer job at Boeing for a career in show business. As a stand up comedian, some nights he was brilliant. Other nights, he'd bomb just like the rest of us.

Regardless, we all thought Bill was fiercely quirky and we hired him as a part time writer/performer on our NBC television show, *Almost Live*. He would come to the pitch meetings, make us laugh, and usually persuade us to put his funnier ideas on the air. His character *Speed Walker*, a fast walking crime fighter, was hilarious.

But there was something else quite odd about Bill. We noticed that a lot of his source material came from the various science and trade magazines that kept falling out of his worn backpack. This guy was reading science magazines for fun! Naturally, a room full of comedians gave him endless grief about it.

Soon, we would find a way to exploit it.

One day, Geraldo Rivera had to cancel an appearance on our show, due to the flu. That meant we had an emergency six-minute guest slot to fill.

In desperation, I turned to Bill and pleaded, *"Look, if we put you in a lab coat, could you do some kind of funny demonstration?"* He looked around the room, smiling, and said, *"Yeah, I could do something funny with a tub of Liquid Nitrogen."* Frankly, I didn't even know if liquid nitrogen was legal but we had a show to put on so I kept riffing. *"I'll introduce you as Bill Nye, our local science correspondent...no wait, I'll call you Bill Nye, The Science Guy. It'll be great!"*

That night, Bill shattered a liquid-nitrogen-dipped onion like it was a piece of glass. He "roasted" marshmallows in the (minus) 325-degree fluid, ate one, and steam blew out of his nose like a dragon!

Hilarious!

Every time Bill made an appearance, he was absolutely hysterical. "Science Rules" became his trademark phrase and we got lots of letters wondering when he was going to be on again. More impressive was that he made our hard core comedy audience actually *care* about science.

The timing and confluence of those events turned out to be the mother lode for Bill. Because he tapped into his passion, Bill became a breakout TV star that could leave his aeronautical day job in the dust.

Bill threw himself into the study of comedy and science and created an Emmy Award winning TV series that is shown several times a day—all over this blue planet. He has become the 21st Century Mr. Wizard!

To this day, teachers still refer to his monthly newsletter and consult his web site in their classrooms. (www.Nyelabs.com)

But Bill would probably tell you his greatest personal accomplishment came when he was asked to join the NASA *Mars Team*. A lifelong lover of outer space, Bill came up with the idea that each of the two Mars Rovers (*Odyssey* and *Spirit*) should have a small sundial attached to their forward panels. That way, kids on earth could see what time it was on Mars.

His instincts were right.

The web site gets thousands of hits a day.

Why the sundial? Or the "Earth dial," as Bill dubbed it.

This is a touching story. Bill's father, Ned, introduced Bill to science through the sundial. During World War II, Ned Nye was a prisoner of war and would put a stick in the sand to keep track of time. So, as a tribute to his father, (who is no longer with us) Bill put two sundials on the planet Mars.

I would challenge you to watch for your own "Bill Nye" within your organization. I'd wager that you are inadvertently wasting the outside talents of your co-workers. Everyone is harboring hidden talents that could be put to use for your company; talents that would yield enormous profits and productivity. Start noticing what magazines your people read and what they do in their off time. Their reading, their TV watching habits, and their web surfing sites will give you a window into their true passions. Allow them to exercise their natural talents and passions at work and you'll not only experience a burgeoning revenue stream but you'll create company ambassadors your customers will love.

REWRITE YOUR MISSION STATEMENT INTO A "PURPOSE" STATEMENT

There is another practical reason to unearth people's talents and interests. Those talents and interests are an expressway to their own feeling of "purpose." You will lose good people if you aren't recognizing what really makes them tick. And your customers will suffer the indifference these disgruntled people will subconsciously transmit.

Most experts agree that 66% of employees leave a job because of poor treatment by their supervisor. Poor treatment can mean everything from, "The boss was a screaming, sexist taskmaster" to "I'm not getting enough recognition for my work."

In Daniel Pink's book, *Free Agent Nation*, he estimates that 32 million Americans work for themselves in a one or two person business. 32 million is a significant population number considering the entire "public sector" is only 21 million.

A great many of these people said they left managers who didn't acknowledge their true talents and "didn't reinforce a sense of purpose." The overwhelming majority of them said they didn't leave bad companies.

They left bad managers.

These "micro-preneurs" got fed up with glacial corporate decision-making, too many layers of managerial protocol, and decided to follow their hearts to create a niche business they felt could make a difference in people's lives. Doing that gave them a sense of purpose. Because we spend so much time at work, we want to feel like our time is being spent doing something worthwhile.

Keep in mind that the opposite behavior isn't transparent. Customers can tell when your employee's "heart isn't in the work." And if your employees don't care about your company, why should your customers?

PURPOSE SURFACES—IF YOU JUST PAY ATTENTION

I met a Las Vegas software engineer named Brett Williams. Brett told me, "I think I was born to train dogs...particularly team sport dogs. In fact, our team is world class in *Fly Ball*." Brett starts training them the second he gets off work—and both weekend days. He feels great about using his time and talents in pursuit of his purpose. He's says he gets "so jazzed" about this, that when he's training his dogs, he never looks at the clock. And because Brett is so passionate about his "second job," his team is ranked #2 in the world in *Fly Ball* competition.

Check out the *New York Times* Best seller book list and you'll see the blistering popularity of purpose. Purpose is the focus of books like, *Purpose Driven Life* (What On Earth Am I Here For?) by Rick Warren, *What Should I Do With My Life?* By Po Bronson, *The Five People You Meet in Heaven* by Mitch Albom, to name a few. All of these books try to answer the meaning of life and what some people, here on earth, are doing about it.

Regretfully, most business managers do a horrible job of informing their employees about the company's real purpose. Worse, they don't tell the employee how his/her particular talents help drive that purpose within the company. For example, if you manufacture cardboard boxes, don't post a mission statement that says,

---

MISSION STATEMENT:

"We want to be the most profitable cardboard box company in the world."

A statement like that doesn't make an emotional statement about the work a person does. It doesn't enrich anybody's soul. Besides that, it's an Inside-Out view of your company. It's your proclamation. You decided this is what you want to be and now you will everything within your power to make it come true. But the final arbiters of your success are your customers. What if they don't want what you have? What if you don't deliver your goods and services they way they want them? A mission statement may end up being a distorted view of how the the world sees you.

Ask yourself the tougher questions. Why are you performing this service or making these products? Who are your customers? Are you needed? Are you wanted? Why do you exist? What *purpose* does your company and your employees serve in the world. Look at your organization from the Outside-In and create a purpose statement.

PURPOSE STATEMENT

"Our purpose is to make reliable cardboard boxes so that others can ship enough food to feed a nation. The boxes you cut ship medicine and life saving equipment to hospitals. Our boxes bring music and laughter to millions of people every day. People will use our boxes to safely move their treasured belongings from one home to another. In every case, we want our customers to be able to rely on the quality and strength of our product; to make their lives easier. You are an important person who helps make all of this happen."
Thank you for being here.

Now, wouldn't that make a person feel better about scoring and assembling cardboard boxes?

Whenever I speak to a business organization, I want to understand what these people are really doing at work. I want to know exactly how 'what they do' affects the rest of us. What cog are they in my overall wheel of life?

Employees need to know that what they do, matters. They need to be reminded that they make someone else's life easier, happier, tastier, prettier, more convenient, or more organized.

EVEN HOSTESS TWINKIES HAVE A PURPOSE.

I went through the Hostess Twinkie plant in Seattle a few years ago and the floor manager made every assembly line worker feel important. I saw him walk over to the assembly line; where literally hundreds of Twinkies were dancing down the conveyer belt like the chocolate factory scene from *I Love Lucy*. He smiled at his crew, grabbed his stomach with both hands, and said, *"Yummmmy! I wish I could see the grin on someone's face when they break the seal on that little yellow cake. They may've had a hard day or were looking forward to a relaxing lunch. You all are packaging a four inch long spongy vacation for those people. When they bite into that Twinkie filling, we're gonna lower stress out there."*

It's up to each of us to know what makes us feel purposeful in our lives. It's up to management to make sure employees understand the purpose of your goods and services. Make people feel good about what they do and you'll have no trouble keeping them on staff.

WHO'S WITH YOU...AND WHO'S AGAINST YOU?

I was the Master of Ceremonies for a Motorola executive conference a couple years ago and I heard Marcus Buckingham shock the leadership team with data from the Gallup Organization. Marcus is a former Senior VP of the Gallup Organization. He and co-author Curt Coffman wrote, *First, Break All The Rules,* and have popularized the terms "employee engagement" and "customer engagement." Marcus told this group,

> *"We studied 80,000 managers from 400 companies and found that only 26% of employees were actively engaged in trying to make the company better. Engaged employees know how they fit into the organization and they feel that their talents are being used on the job. They are also great champions of the business. They have an emotional connection to the company. The largest group, 55%, were not engaged. These people did what was required of them but nothing else. These people didn't have an emotional connection to the company. In fact, they*

*could be quite negative when it came to
expressing their views about how the company
should be run. But by far the most alarming
statistic was that 19% of the employees were
actively disengaged. These people actually work
against their own company. They hate change
and are very dangerous to your business."*

Hmmm, which group do you think cares most about the customer?

Here's a hint.

It is impossible for unhappy people to make other people happy.

If what Buckingham and Coffman is true (and I believe it is) then we need to do whatever we can to move the *not engaged* and *actively disengaged* people into the top tier; the *engaged group.*

If employees are excited about, and believe in the company, they will automatically telegraph their enthusiasm and authenticity to the customer. It follows that customers want to do business with people who care.

Do your people care? How can you find out?

In, *First Break All The Rules,* Buckingham and Coffman write that the most productive, longest tenured, and most engaged employees could answer 'Yes" to the following six questions.

(1) Do I know what is expected of me at work?

(2) Do I have the materials and equipment I need to do my work right?

(3) Do I have the opportunity to do what I do best every day?

(4) In the last seven days, have I received recognition or praise for good work?

(5) Does my supervisor, or someone at work, seem to care about me as a person?

(6) Is there someone at work who encourages my development?

If you are a leader who wants to know if your people are truly charged up and enthusiastic, have them take a stab at that list.

THE BEST INCENTIVE SYSTEM I'VE EVER SEEN

Straight talking Larry Bossidy, former superstar CEO of Honeywell and co-author of, Execution and Confronting Reality, confided in me that, *"A lot of companies think the way to reach stretch goals is to put higher rewards on their performance numbers. But that doesn't enhance your culture. We have to reward them for their behavior...and how they reinforce the company culture. If the culture is united, the numbers will follow."*

Well, I met a car company that kicked that notion up a notch.

Dornett Wright is the HR manager for *DaimlerChrysler Services Truck Finance.* Of all the companies I've had the privilege to see from the inside out, this group is doing something truly groundbreaking. Compensation is tied to several relevant factors.

- Performance numbers and goals

- Behaviors supporting the culture and mission statement

- Customer responses to their efforts
- Suggesting bright new ideas
- Personal career development

The company gets everything it wants in reaching goals and encouraging cultural behavior. And the employee gets customer feedback and the opportunity to submit bright ideas. But the fresh element is the prospect for personal career development.

This is revolutionary stuff!

This is the solution you've been looking for to improve the focus and productivity of your younger workforce. A program that helps workers discover their strengths and talents...will hold their attention and nurture their desire to find fulfilling work. This program doesn't refer to just college extension courses. A lot of companies do that. No, Daimler-Chrysler Services has a program called, *Career Partnership,* that empowers each person to help find the right job for themselves. Through personality testing, goal setting classes, learning how to "chart your own course," and assigning a career coach, this company encourages each person "to find their strengths." Wright told me,

A lot of young people don't know what they want to do, yet. Career Partnership allows them to identify their passion, skill sets and developmental steps. We provide access to global career opportunities within the family of DaimlerChrysler companies and we want our employees to know we value their contributions.

Richard A. Howard, Vice President, DaimlerChrysler Services Truck Finance, describes their philosophy (and responsibility) of maintaining happy, productive employees—and the ensuing customer result.

"Customer focus is one of our core values and defines who we are as a company worldwide. Customer focus means to take care of the needs of our internal customers—our employees—and our external customers who purchase our products and services. Take care of your customers and they will take care of you."

This is a company that recognizes a strong corporate foundation (and sustained profit) springs from the value of putting the right people in the right jobs. So, it's no wonder that Daimler/Chrysler is blowing the proverbial car doors off Ford and General Motors.

HIRE TALENTS; NOT RESUMES

When you hire new people, forget what the glow-in-the-dark resume says.

What kind of personality does it take to do the job? Outgoing? Creative? Focused? Tough?

What talents are required? Competitive nature? Numbers cruncher? Charismatic salesperson?

DON'T FALL PREY TO BAD "CASTING"

Managers should think of themselves as movie producers.

In movie making, the first rule of casting characters (in a comedy, for example) is to "hire funny people." I like Sly Stallone but he isn't a naturally funny movie character. If you ever saw his dreadful "comedic" performance in *Oscar*, you know what I mean. But if you want to hire a convincing, tough, dramatic actor, check out Stallone in *Copland*.

Superb.

"Casting" people for their talents and strengths is how you'll get the best performance out of your actors. I have no idea why most managers haven't caught on to the idea of good casting. Time pressure must certainly be a factor. They have a job to fill and they need to do it quickly. So, they look for resume "skills" rather than human "talent." It's a costly mistake. In the movie business, if a director (manager) hires "against type," the production is usually a flop.

So, stop hiring by the resume and start hiring by the natural talents that can create emotional loyalty in your customers.

If your business depends upon talking to people to make the sale, don't hire people who would rather squirrel themselves away in a dark room generating graphs and spreadsheets. Hire people who are naturally prone to putting people at ease in a conversation, are friendly to strangers, able to show empathy, are curious, caring, alert, energetic, enthusiastic, initiating, and responsible.

Too often, managers don't think to look for the emotional strengths. Those are the talents that perpetuate the customer-centric culture. Those are the traits of people who can build and maintain relationships. Those people don't need to be reminded to be repeat niceties. It's in their nature. A good "service attitude" lives within that person wherever he/she goes. These people are invaluable to you because they can hit the ground running in any job and any position change; regardless of the stalled (or active) state of "training."

Most importantly, those people can turn one-time patrons into loyal customers who love you.

Incidentally, you can also teach those people to create spreadsheets. But you can't hire smart people and then teach them to be human.

STOP HIRING SELF CENTERED PEOPLE FOR A CUSTOMER-CENTRIC ORGANIZATION

I often see this happen in sales organizations. Sales managers like to hire people with "healthy egos" because they think self confidence allows that person to "take charge and own" a territory. But, smart managers are cautious of the difference between being self confident and being self absorbed. It's very hard to teach customer service to self centered people. Their world revolves around themselves. They don't care much for other people except for what other people can do for *them.*

Is there any way to convert the self-absorbed?

You *can* get self centered people to *act* interested and eventually change their behaviors (to fit your customer service culture) *if* you can show them it's in their best financial interest to do so. Sometimes repeating an uncomfortable behavior laced with a reward can actually change the original behavior. However, from my experience, you can't be subtle with self centered people.

Be blunt.

Pull that person aside privately and say, *"You talk too much about yourself. Consider listening more. Try showing more interest in other people for a month and let's see how it affects your numbers."*

What if it's the boss who is self centered? What if you want to champion your brilliant idea because you know it will work—but the boss won't listen?

Larry Bossidy told me, *"If you are on the bottom of an organization and you want to submit an idea to a pig-headed boss, the best way to get the boss to listen is to show him how your idea will serve his best interest. The boss is under pres-*

sure to perform, too. Show him how to beat his sales numbers or increase his stock price, and he'll listen."

MANAGERS, PLEASE TAKE YOUR TIME

Most managers I meet are impatient. They want to fill the position quickly so they can "keep the machinery moving"—without mining the hidden talents they may already have in their current human inventory.

Managers will complain, "Good people are hard to find" (never a good excuse) so they tend to hire "by the pulse." Or, managers will send a likely candidate through a battery of interviews and personality tests...and still end up putting the wrong person in the wrong job.

Another trap is hiring someone...just like *you*. Be wary of hiring clones. A clone will only give you your ideas back to you. As I heard best selling author and Pastor Rick Warren say, *"When two people agree on everything, one of you isn't necessary."*

Also, don't hire a person to fill a temporary position until something better opens up. The manager may say, "I know this isn't an immediate fit but I need you to do this other thing for a little while until we can find something more suitable for you."

What?!

Do you think your "new hire" will be productive, at a job they don't want, until Mr. Manager can find something better for them?

Here's what can happen if you rush the hiring process.

When we moved to our new house, I had to change phone companies. So, I called to make an appointment for installation. After I suffered through the various menus prompts, I finally reached a dull and unenthusiastic male voice that droned...

"hi....thank you for calling (XXX). my name is Jason. how may i provide you with outstanding customer service?"

(I intentionally used lower case letters to emphasize how lackluster his performance was).

Now, why would any company, let alone a phone company, (1) demand that a representative repeats such an obviously contrived salutation, and (2) how did Jason ever get a job answering phones in the first place?! This was the first, and most important, impression I would have with the company and I was lucky enough to locate their most disengaged employee.

I told him he could best help me by quitting that job.

Our cell phone carrier isn't any better. They don't even bother to say *Hello* when you call.

The following conversation actually occurred.

(THE CONNECTION CLICKS THROUGH)

PHONE COMPANY: May I have your account number?

ROSS: 182LH30XX

PHONE COMPANY: Who am I speaking with?

ROSS: Ross Shafer

PHONE COMPANY: What are the last four digits of your Social Security number?

ROSS: XXXX

PHONE COMPANY: Yes, that's correct. (her mood shifts) How are you doing today Mr. Shafer?

Apparently, they will only be nice to you once they determine you are a qualified customer.

We need to get mad and hold management accountable for inventing that stupid sequence of asking for account information *before* saying "Hello" to the customer. Then, indict that manager for hiring someone dumb enough to carry out that ridiculous edict.

EVERY JOB HAS THE ABILITY TO DERAIL YOUR ORGANIZATION

Managers tend to neglect the lower echelon positions because they don't see a direct revenue stream coming from these people.

I went to my bank to deposit a check at the ATM and the parking lot security guard came up to me and said, *"You can't park your car there. That's the manager's slot."*

Why would a bank hire a person to make the first customer greeting so harsh?

The bank needed security but didn't consider what a critical role that person played in the total experience.

So, I will shout it now.

THE SECURITY GUARD IS YOUR TALKING BILLBOARD. IF THEY ARE THE FIRST PEOPLE TO REPRESENT YOU. MAKE THEM FEEL IMPORTANT.

Receptionists also fall into this category. They have the first responsibility to attract business in person and/or on the phone. Receptionists are the unseen (but loudly heard) 'experience conduit' for the rest of your company. Hire friendly, warm, engaging, empathetic, patient people for this position. Hire people who naturally smile when they pick up the phone. Hire people who ask your permission before they "transfer you." Customers don't like to be silently clicked into voice menu oblivion.

Call your company (as if *you* were a new customer) and listen to how you are being represented. It may make you want to run down and answer the phone yourself.

EVERYBODY HAS BAD DAYS, BUT...

Of course we all have bad days. But every contact can either improve or destroy our foundation of trust and goodwill with them.

Remind your people that even when they are having a bad day they have a responsibility to *not* think about themselves. Always realize that the day is not about *your* glory. Your customer's feeling come first and they are coming to you with their own inventory of vulnerability, helplessness, fear, and anxiety. We can carry on with our own bad day during our lunch hour or when we get home. But "on the clock" we owe the customer our best performance.

CHAPTER 7

BIG CHANGE #3
CUSTOMERS WANT YOU TO "READ THEIR MINDS"

How can we read a customer's mind? By eliminating the practice of training *the position*—and replacing it with training people in the art of humanity. And, I'm talking about both kinds of customers. External and internal.

Humanity is the trap door to your customer's mind.

Humanity is also the most effective employee motivator.

Look at your own organization. It's an emotionally charged moving target; with customers whose tastes can change at the same rate.

Companies are merging, growing, shrinking, and globalizing at an ever accelerating rate.

"Change" has become too slow a word!

Employees barely get the ink dry on their business cards before their duties and responsibilities become obsolete.

CURRENT TRAINING METHODS ARE TEMPORARY

In the "soft skills" training business (as opposed to hard issues training like Sexual Harassment, Diversity, Compliance, and Safety) we have been constantly reminding workers to have fun, be nice to people, and reminding them that the customer is the most important element of our business. It must be or we wouldn't inscribe those words on our Mission Statements.

And to hold our employees attention, we've tried to make training fun.

John Cleese, of Monty Python fame, raised the bar in the training field by forming a company called *Video Arts*. His training films weren't just talking heads in front of a phony office setting. They were clever and funny. His film, *Meetings, Bloody Meetings*, made the training experience more like watching *Saturday Night Live*. In fact, training videos became popular because many of them were similar to watching a TV show. One of the most popular (and funny) customer training films ever produced was called *The Guest*; produced by *Media Partners, Inc.* In fact, when you visit a hotel or restaurant and they refer to you as a "guest" it's largely because this film popularized that term. *Remember Me?* is also a perennial training favorite—as is former restaurateur, Bob Farrel's *Give 'Em The Pickle*. I dare say our film, *Many Happy Returns*, ranks up there with the best of them. But, the blockbuster of all time is *Fish! Fish!* was shot at the Pike Place Fish Market in Seattle, Washington. Legend has it that the film sat dormant for a year before anyone at *Chart House Learning* (the producer) had enough confidence to release it. Surprisingly, *Fish!* isn't (technically) a customer service training movie. The story demonstrates how this fresh fish company differentiates itself by having fun and placing value on the customer.

But even with these marvelous training tools, training people to be customer-service-oriented still has a major problem.

Not enough employees are watching the films.

Drew Hedgcock, owner of Video Training, Inc. and distributor of more than a thousand training movies says,

> *"Prior to 1998, trainers had money to spend on training products. A big chain might call us up and order 200 copies of a training video; one for each location. But since 911, budgets have been very tight. Now, a large company with several hundred outlets will call us and only buy one tape. Can you guess how long it would take to train three thousand people with a single video tape?"*

My guess would be about 16 years!

When revenues are down, the first department to get cut is the customer service training department—the one department that can put instant money in the company kitty.

Beyond budget restraints, training employees gets bogged down in the muddy waters of a merger.

Hedgcock told me,

> *"You would think a merger would be good for the training business. I mean, here are two*

companies getting together who you would think would want to simultaneously educate everyone—bring the two cultures together like a team. But that's not what happens. I'll call an HR Director to tell her about a new show I think might fit her situation and she'll tell me that she can't do any training now because she doesn't know if she will have a job when the dust settles. And she'll say, 'If I do have a job, I'll have to rewrite the training objectives to suit the new culture. So, I don't even know what to buy to train people."

Regardless of the state of the workforce, commerce must refuse to grind to a halt over the training and retraining process. Succumb to that and your profits grind to a halt in tandem.

Let's not forget that customers are still standing in line to buy goods and services. And, these customers still want excellent treatment.

So let's agree that we, as trainers, and you as managers and front line staff, need to stop training people in traditional ways. Let's focus on training their humanity. Let's stop telling them to behave alike—and instead, let's draw out their individual human strengths. Let's teach our people to get to know other people. Humanity skills will transcend any structural change and every merger upheaval.

TRAIN EMPLOYEES TO BE NON-VERBAL EXPERTS

Reading the customer's mind wasn't a metaphor. You can really learn to do it. The reason it's so important to have non-verbal skills is because most all of our interactions begin without words.

Before they come to you, your customer has been living a whole other life full of routine and surprises. You can't predict their state of mind by the time they get to you. But, if you can learn to read the emotions of your customers—those hidden messages they aren't verbalizing—you'll find the quickest shortcut to your customer's heart.

Also, keep in mind that the customer takes cues from your reactions and behaviors. So, let's review the emotional effect your words and actions have on a customer.

> When a sales person doesn't smile at a customer, the customer *feels disliked.*

> If the sales associate doesn't make eye contact, the customer *feels unimportant.*

> When a clerk doesn't acknowledge a customer, they *feel rejected.*

> When a clerk uses foul language within earshot of the customer, they feel *disrespected, embarrassed,* and *possibly angry.*

"READING PEOPLE" CAN BE AS EASY AS BREATHING

Reading a customer's mind is not impossible. The clues are written all over their faces.

Face reading is used by well known jury consultants like Jo-Ellen Dimitrius, Phd, the author of *Reading People.* She and others, in her profession, earn substantial fees by interpreting facial expressions. You can imagine how, without talking to a prospective juror, she has to be able to recommend the twelve best decision makers who will most likely influence her client's legal outcome. Based on her talents for reading faces, vocal inflections and body language, she can make critical judgments about a prospective juror's moods, state of mind, and how they may vote in what could be a life or death decision for a specific defendant.

Face reading is also crucial for award winning *National Geographic* photographers like Christopher Johns (now Associate Editor in Chief) and David Alan Harvey. Chris told me about one of his assignments in the remote tribal lands of New Guinea. He wasn't unable to communicate by language. But he *was* able to rely on his knowledge of facial expressions to know whether or not they would be cooperative photographic subjects.

MIND READING IS THE BEST "LIFE SKILL" YOU CAN TEACH

I was teaching extension classes at the University of Washington, on executive public speaking, and I frequently talked about 'reading the faces of your audience.' Every stage performer watches for signals that will tell him/her, "I've got them in the palm of my hand," or "Uh oh, I think I've lost them." One day, a faculty member audited my class and said I should check out a psychology professor on campus named John Gottman. Well, this man has made an intricate science out of face reading. Among his 36 books, Gottman offers practical applications for this skill in his tomes, *The Mathematics of Divorce,* and *The Seven Principles for Making Marriage Work; Why Marriages Succeed or Fail...and How You Can Make Yours Last.*" So exacting is his research that he can watch a husband and wife interact, for under an hour, and frighteningly predict (about 95% of the time) whether or not the couple will still be married after 15 years.

How can he do that?

After studying and videotaping thousands of couples, he has found clear statistical patterns, within facial expressions, that indicate trouble in a marriage. It doesn't take Gottman long to identify the long term marriage killers like disgust, contempt, defensive behaviors, sadness, and "stuffed" anger.

Wouldn't you like to know if your customers are coming to you as happy, frustrated, or sad?

What if you knew your customer was scared? Angry? Reluctant? Irritated...even before they said a single word to you?

If you were able to correctly read faces, you would know how to respond to any customer and in any situation.

What do you watch for?

Watch the size of the eyes, the open or closed mouth, the tilt of the head, and what the body is doing. Aggressive expressions like anger and disgust cause the body to lean forward. Fear and sadness are regressive and tend to cause people to lean back. Even in barking dogs, the noise may be loud but the position of their legs is low and bent backward; allowing them a fast retreat. Other strong indicators are the size and direction of the eyes—as well as the tension of the lips and mouth. Tight lips indicate disgust and anger—while a relaxed mouth can indicate either happiness or fear.

FACE READING...*THE SCIENCE*

Reading faces (Physiognomy is the official name) was an ancient art practiced by the likes of Aristotle and Plato. Even modern day financial guru, Charles Schwab, is a fan of physiognomy and councils others on how to find the right job using these techniques. Face reading is real and respected.

I once saw an incredible demonstration of face reading by Mac Fulfer. Mac Fulfer is an attorney and the author of *Amazing Face Reading* (www.amazingfacereading.com). He is an ardent practitioner of this art and makes perfect sense when he says,

> *"Life events shape our face. Or put another way, our face is shaped by the way we use it. We readily accept that we can change our bodies. If we want bigger muscles we sign up for a health club, and we are not surprised when we see results." "Yet we seldom stop to consider that our faces are just as changeable. For example, if you are a person who requires of yourself a forced mental focus as a habitual pattern, you will develop those vertical lines you can see between the eyebrows."*

Fulfer implores his students to notice that faces are not symmetrical. Each half has its own "personality." How can that be? The right side of the brain (non-linear, imaginative side) controls the left side of the body and face. The left side (linear, logical side) controls the right side of the body and face. Furthermore, the left side of the face (right brain) represents the person's personal and "inner" life while the right side of the face (left brain) represents the business and "outside world" life.

It follows that if the linear side of your brain is constantly under more stress than the creative side of your brain, your mind will "exercise" the right side of your body in a different way. Over time, it will develop different lines and muscles.

When it comes to reading your customer's faces, Fulfer has a simple test to judge if the customer is open to you or "closed off."

Go to a mirror and look at your eyes. More specifically, look at the whites of your eyes. If you see white on the bottom of the iris but not on the top, that person's brow is bearing down on the eyes. This is a sign of stress. You can be a great relief to this customer by showing empathy and helping them through a difficult decision.

If you see white above the iris—but not on the bottom—that person is about to "lose it." According to Fulfer, this is a person who is about to reach their psychological flight-or-fight threshold.

However, if you see white all around the iris, this person is in extreme mental disconnect. This person doesn't want to be here and may not even be aware of his actions. You'll have to do most of the work in this transaction.

Now for the eyelids.

If the customer's eyes are squinted and only allow a sliver of the eye to show, this person is skeptical and guarded. This indicates an emotional distance between the two of you. Your best bet is to create trust as quickly as possible.

If the customer's eyelids seem relaxed and open (curved) this person is receptive and non-judgmental. This person is willing to listen to your ideas.

Finally, if the eyelids are drawn down to cover the top half of the pupil, Fulfer says this is a person with a hidden agenda. Proceed with caution.

While you may not have thousands of hours to document every facial expression like Dr. Gottman or Mac Fulfer, you can certainly practice and learn the most important six.

The following "top six" expressions transcend language barriers and cross cultural boundaries in all human beings.

ANGER

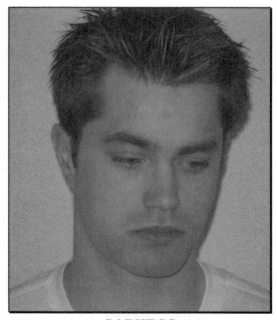

SADNESS

Happiness

Disgust

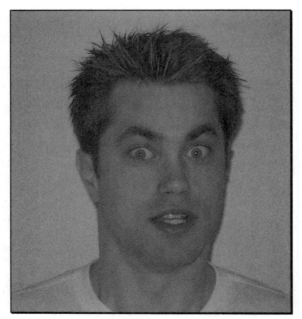

Fear

Contempt

Want to refine your skills? Get some co-workers together and play an emotional guessing game. Write down a list of emotions (one per card) and ask them to demonstrate their facial expressions for each emotion. Then, challenge each other to identify the "mood."

Irritated	Sarcastic	Frustrated
Jealous	Insanely Angry	Smoldering
Disoriented	Confused	Hurt
Sneaky	Deceptive	False confidence

You get the idea.

Reading people's faces is something you can practice at the supermarket, a night club, a soccer game, in a school class, at a cocktail party, and anywhere people are interacting with other people. The more you practice this skill, the more successful you'll be in your work and personal life—with far fewer misunderstandings with people.

> SIDE NOTE: My assistant, Caryn Stanley, read this chapter and had a profound and relevant question. She said, "I wonder if a recent Botox treatment could cause a misinterpretation?" Yes! In fact, I've heard that it's common for contestants in professional poker tournaments to get Botox injections, before a big match, to hide their "tells."

READING PEOPLE HAS AN AWESOME SIDE EFFECT

By reading other people, you will stop thinking about *yourself*.

Self centered people are typically terrible at empathy and reading people. They believe that only *their* feelings matter.

If this is you, start focusing your attention on other people's feelings and you'll be more sensitive to the world around you. You will accidentally become more interesting and attract more people to you.

Don't talk so much. Listen more. Someone very smart once said, *"You never learn anything when you are talking."* When someone talks, ask a follow-up question. Don't jump right in with, *"Hey, that reminds ME of something that happened to ME."*

JOHNNY CARSON WAS AN EMPATHY MASTER

The late Johnny Carson once said to me, "You will do fine (in the talk show business) if you remember that the show isn't all about you. You don't have to be the best guest on your own show." Johnny Carson was an expert at reading people. He knew when to ask questions. And he knew when to shut up and let people talk. I heard him tell Barbara Walters, "The best thing a talk show host can have going for him (or her) is curiosity." Let other people talk. Learn something about someone else. I learned early on that if you want to create quick rapport with someone, ask people about themselves. So many times, when I have been at a party, in my "interview mode," (i.e.; asking all the questions) the subject would tell me, "I can tell you were a talk show host. You're a wonderful conversationalist."

See what I mean?! People will think you are a great conversationalist if you ask questions about *them.*

What's ironic is that when I started in television (in 1983), it was a commonly held view that women didn't make good talk show hosts because they didn't have the authority of a man's physical presence and voice.

What a crock!

The world's most successful talk show host—in the entire history of talk shows—is Oprah Winfrey. To my knowledge, no man has ever accumulated a billion dollars in net worth hosting talk shows. Oprah is successful because she listens. She has boundless empathy. She can read people. She's curious. And, her viewers appreciate her abilities because she mirrors their own interests and frailties.

Oprah exudes humanity.

TEACH PEOPLE TO BE VERBALLY 'CONSCIOUS"

I worry about a younger generation that has become so brilliantly nimble at text messaging that they are losing the ability to communicate in person. Many of them have no idea how to choose the best words to encourage, the best words to critique, and how the wrong words at the wrong time can destroy their careers, as well as your business.

So, it's up to you to train them in this interactive skill; a skill they can carry with them for a lifetime.

THE WRONG WORDS CAN DESTROY MORALE & STRANGLE YOUR PROFITS

When you were in grade school and someone called you a derogatory or insulting name, it hurt your feelings. Our parents would try to make us feel better by saying, *"Sticks and stones may break your bones but words will never hurt you."*

But that's a lie.

Your initial reaction was the truth.

Your feelings were hurt.

Words have enormous power to destroy the attitudes of your employees and your customers.

John Bargh, of NYU and Stanford, is one of a group of psychology professors who are interested in learning how our moods and behaviors change by the subconscious things we see and hear. Bargh and his team design experiments with a hidden contextual message. He calls them "priming experiments." A priming experiment misdirects the subject into thinking the experiment is about one thing—when the real experiment has been manipulated to produce the true subconscious reaction. How can priming experiments help you? They can demonstrate how the right and wrong subconscious words can trigger a person's conscious behaviors.

Malcolm Gladwell, in his book *Blink*, describes one such John Bargh word experiment.

"Imagine that I'm a professor, and I've asked you to come to see me in my office. You walk down a long corridor, come through the doorway, and sit down at a table. In front of you is a sheet of paper with a list of five-word sets. I want you to make a grammatical four-word sentence as quickly as possible out of each set. It's called a scrambled-sentence test. Ready?

01 him was worried she always
02 from are Florida oranges temperature
03 ball the throw toss silently
04 shoes give replace old the
05 he observes occasionally people watches
06 be will sweat lonely they
07 sky seamless gray is
08 should now withdraw forgetful we

09 us bingo sing play let
10 sunlight makes temperature wrinkle raisins

That seemed straightforward, right? Actually, it wasn't.

After you finished that test—believe it or not—you would have walked out of my office and back down the hall more slowly than you walked in. With that test, I affected the way you behaved. How? Well, look back at the list.

Scattered throughout it are certain words, such as "worried," "Florida," "old," "lonely," "gray," "bingo," and "wrinkle." You thought I was just making you take a language test, But, in fact, what I was also doing was making the big computer in your brain—your adaptive unconscious—think about the state of being old. It didn't inform the rest of your brain about its sudden obsession. But it took all this talk about old age so seriously that by the time you finished and walked down the corridor, you acted old. You walked slowly."

I was so intrigued by the idea that we could affect behavior with a "hidden context" that I secretly experimented with one of my seminar audiences.

There were 75 people in the meeting room. I set up two video cameras; one in the back of the room to ostensibly videotape my performance. The other camera was set up in the front of the room; trained on the audience. I told them I only wanted to tape them to use as a cut-a-way shot if I needed to edit the "master" shot later.

The morning session went as I'd planned. Then, we broke for lunch. About 20 minutes after lunch I introduced my own "priming experiment" (by now they had forgotten about the cameras). I recorded the audience's posture prior to the experiment. Picture a room full of people after lunch—stuffed with food and a bit logy. While I am considered to be an animated and enthusiastic speaker, I'll admit that some of the people were starting to slump and stifle their burps. My set up context was: "If we use the right words in our communication we can cut down on mistakes and misunderstandings." As a demonstration, I asked them to fill out a quick "language skills" test.

Again, make a four word phrase out of the five scrambled words. The phrase does not have to make a complete sentence.

01 Season joyous a Christmas holiday

02 Wandering boundless have children energy

03 Can baby always happy a

04 Tall pick peaches young never

05 Project was design the vibrant

06 People easy longer wealthy live

When I looked at the tape after the meeting, I found that Bargh was right.

I'm a rank amateur at priming experiments...but all I had to do was hide the words *joyous, energy, happy, young, vibrant,* and *wealthy*—and the effect on the attendee's state-of-mind was immediate and obvious. Because the hidden words were associated with "youth," the videotape clearly showed that the same logy-looking people in the audience changed their posture from slouchy to erect. People became more alert and bubbly. Where they had been quiet and private during the first experiment...they now chatted and laughed amongst themselves trying to make funny combinations with the words. When I explained what I had done, not one person guessed the pattern or connection of the words. Yet, most all of them manifested the effect. I've repeated this demonstration with several audiences; in vastly different parts of the United States. The results are always the same. Old, tired words make people feel old and tired. Young, vibrant words make people feel young and vibrant.

You could say that magicians are regular practitioners of priming experiments. They call it "the misdirection play" and the power of suggestion. They get you to focus on the left hand while the right hand steals your wristwatch. They "suggest" an outcome and somehow it comes true. Now, apply the same power of suggestion (in a negative way) to your workplace and watch what happens. Can you see how quickly our subconscious mind can absorb (and change) your behaviors. Imagine what a destructive effect can take place in an environment rife with gossip, bad language, complaining, and resentment.

KILL OFFICE POLITICS WHERE IT LIVES

Backstabbing, gossip, and office politics are a cancer for any company. Gossip, true or not, has a debilitating effect that can rage under its own power. In *Nobody Moved Your Cheese!*, I wrote about the *7 Habits of Highly Sneaky People Who Will Screw You*, at work. I'll reprint some of it here because I had so many resonating comments about that chapter.

1) They gossip about your mutual friends behind their backs.

Oh yeah, it's really funny when Darla pulls you aside to gossip about Cathy's disastrous family life. She also makes fun of her vocabulary, her hair style, her clothes, and the loser men she dates. But, you aren't in a secured cone-of-silence with Darla. Darla is saying the same things about you behind your back—probably telling Cathy about your drunken tattoo night. Would she really do that? Yes. People who gossip can't stop. You are tomorrow's gossip and Darla will deny it if you confront her; which is why it won't do you any good to confront her. The solution? Keep gossip to yourself and be too busy to chat with her when Darla calls.

2) They only call you when they need something.

Selfish people couldn't care less about you. They will smile as they use you for advice, to cover their fanny, or curry favor. But the favors are never reciprocal. If backed into a corner, these people won't help you and will not be your ally. They may be the funniest people to invite to your party but they are the weasels who WON'T get out of bed to help you change a flat tire on a stormy night. Try not to get too close to these takers because you will expect too much and always be disappointed.

3) They deliberately misinterpret what you say or lie TO SAVE FACE.

If you get into a jam and your friend deliberately misstates what you know to be the truth, you better know that this person would jerk the rescue rope from your hands to save his/her slippery hide. They will even apologize to you, "I'm sorry. What could I do? I was backed into a corner and I could have lost my job. I'll make it up to you." You're sorry? Me too. One chance is all I give these spineless half-wits.

4) *They build a case against you; cataloguing your mistakes.*

In college, I became friendly with a guy named Mark Dix (a fake name but he will know who he is). We both worked in retail clothing in Yakima, Washington. I later moved to Seattle. We were great buddies and when Mark and his wife, Marta, wanted to move to Seattle, I got him a job at the same store where I was working. Over the next year, he methodically built a fabricated case against me and I got fired. As you can probably imagine, Mark was standing by to take my job. In retrospect, I knew Mark was dishonest and sneaky. He cheated at pool. He cheated on his wife. Other times, he would quiz me over and over about what I was doing. Then, misquote me and use it against me with the boss. Occasionally, I would walk around a corner and catch him in a halting conversation with the boss. But he was my best friend, at the time, and I blindly blew it off. Don't be as dumb as I was. If you get suspicious for good reason, do something about it? There is only one way to stop this sort of thing.
Never make friends with Mark Dix.

5) THEY BUILD ALLIANCES WITH OTHERS TO WEAKEN YOU.

I used to have a joke in my act that went,. "I work at an advertising agency and my co-workers are constantly trying to sabotage me. They keep letting me pitch my own ideas." The joke was borne from truth. My co-workers knew that, at 23, I was weak "on my feet" so they let me hang myself in meetings. My ineptness guaranteed that my corporate rise would spiral clockwise like a flushed toilet. Sure enough, almost anybody got promoted over me.

Were they really jumping over me or was I imagining it? Woody Allen used to say something like, 'Just because you're paranoid, don't let your paranoia convince you that people really aren't out to get you." Hey, if you are feeling left out, you probably are. Like buzzards circling their prey, you are probably the next one to be eaten. The solution is to divide and conquer. If you really care about staying where you are, break up the group. Worm your way into the only good hearted person, in sight, and work your way out from there. Integrity, honesty, and truth are still your strongest weapons.

6) They steal your ideas.

First, there is blatant theft of your sole idea. Then there is team theft. The "team" works together to solve problems, right? So how can it be stealing if the group created the "intellectual property?" I'm talking about someone, on the team, who sees a window of opportunity and deliberately steals your ideas, your plan, your model, you're...whatever... for their personal gain. The major problem is that these jerks have no conscience about doing it. I love their rationale, "Look, it isn't personal. It's just business."

It's always personal when you rob someone's originality and call it your own! And, these people will do it over and over again as a normal way of doing business. If you spot them, change the locks on your brain and never leave a spare key under your toupee.

7) THEY ARE HOT TEMPERED TO THE POINT OF IRRATIONALITY.

This group is scary. They yell. They blow easily and you never know what they will say in the heat of the moment. Most likely, they will spit out whatever is meant to cause immedi-

ate pain; which may be anything you may have uttered in confidence. They may not even mean to shaft you. But they are hotheads and you could inadvertently get caught up in their backwash. How can you fend off the loudmouth and the stupidly opinionated? Keep your thoughts to yourself. Don't give them ammunition that may be damaging or incriminating to you and your career.

Believe it or not, there is good news here. The people described above are at the peak of their careers. Nobody likes them and nobody wants to work with them. They aren't moving up. Competitive companies cannot afford to keep these disengaged people on the payroll because they're not contributing to any of the profits. If you don't do any more than is required of you, you can't grow...because everyone knows you aren't contributing to the growth of the company. Who do you know like this? If you know who they are, disown them. You will do just fine without them. In fact, by discarding them, you can't be found guilty by their slimy association.

CHAPTER 8

BIG CHANGE #4
NEVER FORGET
"THE LEAST YOU
CAN DO"

CUSTOMERS DON'T WANT GOOD CUSTOMER SERVICE ANYMORE

Good isn't good enough.

They want service to be spectacular. But you can't get to spectacular until you deliver "the least you can do."

To review, in *The Customer Talks Back*, customers told us the least you can do is offer:

A SMILE

EYE CONTACT

RESPECT FOR THEIR MONEY & TIME

ATTENTION (JUST ENOUGH)

WELL INFORMED SALES PEOPLE

SMILE & EYE CONTACT (TO THE CUSTOMER) MEANS...

Basic human courtesy.

Customers expect you to be friendly. They want a warm and welcoming experience from you.

Customers expect to see you smile (not frown).

Customers expect you to make eye contact so they fell acknowledged.

RESPECT MEANS...CUSTOMERS DON'T WANT TO BE "DISSED"

Customers want to matter to you.

Customers want you to respect their time, their money, and their experience.

Nobody has enough time. With both members of the household working, customers have so little time to run household errands that many banks have installed mini-branches in grocery stores so that people can combine errands.

Nobody has enough money. Look at your own situation. You are probably doing more work and putting in more hours today than you did five years ago. But, while housing costs, gas prices, food and utility prices have continued to rise, salary levels are, in many cases, (according to the U.S. Dept. of Labor) at 1979 levels. Young couples have to frequently borrow money from their relatives for a down payment on a small condo. Gas prices are so high that, even with stingy, gas-sipping automobiles, many people are forced to carpool to afford the commute. We didn't even have carpool lanes 20 years ago!

Given those financial realities, customers want you to respect the little time they have and the little money they have to spend. Customers don't want to be prejudged on their buying power. In the "trading up" culture shift, your customer may be saving money on less expensive clothes or driving a five year old car so they can afford to spend more money with you.

Customers expect you to keep your promises.

If you say you will do something, they expect you to follow through.

Customers want you to stand behind your goods and services.

In the off-chance something goes wrong, customers want you to be accountable for what you sell.

JUST ENOUGH ATTENTION MEANS...

They want you to offer help if they need it...but not "hover" over them like a vulture waiting for the dinner bell. That means they may want to look (and decide) on their own. That makes a customer feel successful in their choice.

WELL INFORMED SALES PEOPLE MEANS...

Customers expect you to know everything about what you are selling. They want you to be able to answer all of their questions. They expect you to be the expert who can offer unbiased information and a recommendation based on the customer's needs.

HUMANS SHOULD RESPOND TO HUMAN PROBLEMS

Customers complained most about being sent to a web site "support center" to solve their problem. Customers really despise voice mail menus. They don't like being handed off from one menu choice to another...only to finally reach a human being who can't answer their questions. Sophisticated phone system companies can even track which "hand off" caused the customer to get frustrated and hang up. They call it the "customer erosion" point.

Erosion? Let's call it what it is; lost revenue.

Ford Motor Company responded to this issue by yanking out 8,000 land line telephones—and replacing them with cell phones so the customer could have direct access to the engineers.

Citibank ran a commercial during the *2004 World Series* featuring a customer talking to a female cosmetics clerk. Every time the customer tried to ask a question, the clerk would interrupt with a voice menu prompt like, *"For ruby red polish press #1, for fire truck red polish press #2."*

It was pretty funny to see a LIVE clerk mimicking the menu options in front of a LIVE customer. What's not funny is that the scenario is exactly how it feels to the customer. Customers are left with the impression that you think their questions are so mundane that they can be answered by an automated system. The only thing more irritating to the customer is when the company menu "operator" encourages them to visit the company web site's FAQ's (frequently asked questions) page.

More human avoidance.

Customers always feel their situation is unique.

And FYI, customers don't consider an automated email response as "customer service." They only consider it as a receipt.

YOU DON'T GET EXTRA CREDIT FOR BEING RIGHT

Customers expect you to be accurate and not make mistakes. You don't get "extra credit" for being error free. They expect the execution to be flawless.

Customers are paying you for information and expect you to have more answers than they have questions. They need you for that.

CHAPTER 9

BIG CHANGE #5
ACCEPT THAT YOUR
CUSTOMERS ARE
IRRATIONAL.

EMOTIONS OVERRIDE LOGIC

Your great marketing and pricing plans may go sideways at any moment because you can't always predict a customer's motive or logic.

And, don't get mad at them if they change their minds. When they change their minds, they are challenging us to remain relevant.

> TRYING TO UNDERSTAND YOUR CUSTOMER'S EMOTIONS IS IMPORTANT BECAUSE PEOPLE ARE IRRATIONAL.

I met European business guru, Jonas Ridderstrale, at an elite management retreat of only 28 attendees. At six feet tall, dressed in black leather and a shaved head, he's scary looking. He is also considered one of the 50 top thinkers in the world. Jonas and his friend Kjell Nordstrom wrote the book, *Funky Business; Talent Makes Captial Dance.* They claim that emotions can't help but override logic and reason. The limbic region in our brains reacts first to all stimuli. That is the undisputed emotional region of our brains. If you want to activate the central cortex (the logic and reason side) you have to make a conscious decision to apply logic and reason to an emotional issue.

Jonas argues that such an exercise requires that you consciously engage that area of your brain based on your experience and education.

Logical deductions are *not* a natural thought process.

Maybe that's why a psychologist won the Nobel Prize in economics, right?

What? You didn't know that?

A PSYCHOLOGIST WON THE NOBEL PRIZE IN ECONOMICS?

When I first read that Daniel Kahneman had won the 2002 Nobel Prize in economics, I jumped to what I thought was an obvious (but wrong) conclusion.

I assumed he was using psychological models as they related to making financial deals. Like a lot of people, I watch those TV poker tournaments and figured being able to analyze your opponent's weaknesses—being alert to their "tells" probably also works really well in a big business deal.

But that wasn't Kahneman's argument.

Kahneman's win was, *"for having integrated insights from psychological research into economic science, especially concerning human judgment and decision-making under uncertainty."*

Kahenman's "prospect theory" was the first time anyone was able quantify irrationality in business situations. Basically, the idea is that your customers aren't very good at calculating the odds of losing and gaining money...or spending money for that matter. People would rather avoid a loss; regardless of how remote it is, than take a shot at an extremely easy gain.

Colin Camerer, an economist at the California Institute of Technology, in an article titled, *Prospect Theory in the Wild*, talks about how Kahneman's prospect theory applied to New York City cab drivers.

> *"Many New York City cab drivers decide when to finish work each day by setting themselves a daily income target, and on reaching it they stop. This means that they typically work fewer hours on a busy day than on a slow day. Rational labor-market theory predicts that they will do the opposite, working longer on a busy day when their effective hourly wage-rate is higher, and less on the slow day when their wage-rate is lower. Prospect theory can explain this as irrational behavior; failing to achieve the daily income target feels like incurring a loss, so drivers put in longer hours to avoid it, and beating the target feels like a win, so once they have done that, there is less incentive to keep working."*

Camerer gives us a similar example with betting strategy at the horse track. Now, this example lit me up because I worked at the Yakima Valley Race Track as a college student. I've personally watched this psychology in action. Camerer reveals,

"Gamblers tend to shift their bets away from the favorites toward long-shots as the day's racing nears its end. Because of the cut taken by the bookies, by the time later races are run most racegoers have lost some money. For many of them, a successful bet on an outsider would probably turn a losing day into a winning one. Mathematically, and rationally, this should not matter. The last race of the day is no different from the first race of the next day. But most racegoers close their "mental account" at the end of each racing day, and they hate to leave the track a loser."

We see irrational financial behavior all around us.

Is buying a lottery ticket rational...when you know the odds are 23 million-to-one that you will win?

Is pumping quarters into a Las Vegas slot machine rational...on the hope that you win the Dodge Viper on display?

How about investing $10,000 in a high risk Nasdaq traded stock, suggested by your grocery clerk? Is that rational?

At an HR convention, I heard Harvard Professor, Dan Aerily, explain human financial irrationality this way.

"You are shopping for a new computer. It costs $1,000. But if I told you the exact same computer could be bought for $125 cheaper just one block away, would you walk one block to say $125? Most people would say, Yes! But if you were going to buy a new $25,000 car and I told you that the exact same car was $125 cheaper one block away, would you take the walk? Only a small

> *number of people said they would save the*
> *money in the second scenario. Why? It's the same*
> *$125 savings!"*

Advertising has conditioned our customers to think in terms of "percentage of savings." Everyone is excited about an ad or signage that claims, "50–70% OFF!" In the computer example, we saved 12.5%. But in the car example, we only saved .25%—which doesn't seem like enough money saved to walk a block.

But that's not logical, is it? We would still save the same $125 dollars.

We all make dumb, irrational decisions because we're being led around by our emotions. *Every* purchase has the potential to be an emotional transaction for us. Add the pressure of making a decision within a short time frame and the emotional reaction can compound itself. That's why you see so many TV ads that shout, "Prices will only be this low during our 12 hour sale!"—"We are absolutely closing our doors, forever, at midnight!"—and so on. Customers don't react rationally when a sale price is exacerbated by time pressure.

YOUR IRRATIONAL CUSTOMER DRIVES A 'BENZ BUT SHOPS AT WAL*MART?

You probably have irrational financial decision makers in your neighborhood.

Ever heard a millionaire complain about the high cost of gasoline; when they could afford gas if the price was $100 a gallon?

More irrationality, isn't it?

How many of you know someone who spent $55,000 on a Mercedes or BMW but shops for their children's clothes at Wal*Mart?

It's because their decisions are driven by their emotions.

The BMW satisfies the emotion to feel good, successful, or more attractive driving a prestigious car. Yet when they tell you, *"The kids will tear up their clothes anyway so why spend a lot of money on them?"* translates to the emotion; "Look how smart I am!"

In their book, *Trading Up; The New American Luxury,* Michael Silverstein and Neil Fiske talk about the burgeoning American affluence that is causing people to shift their priorities and emotionalize their spending habits.

> *"With 47 million households in the United States with incomes of $50,000 or more, and average household size of 2.6 people, that's nearly 122 million Americans with the means and desire to trade up."*

Silverstein and Fiske cite a great example from an interview they did with a construction worker named Jake. Jake loves golf so much that he works the early shift so he can be on the course at 2:00pm. Jake makes about $50,000 a year.

> *"It took Jake a year to save enough money to buy a complete set of Callaway golf clubs—$3,000 worth of premium titanium-faced drivers, putters, and wedges. Jake says, 'the reason I bought them is that they make me feel rich. You can run the biggest company in the world and be one of the richest guys in the world, but you can't buy any clubs better than these."*

Expensive golf clubs made Jake *feel* rich. That's highly emotional. While spending nearly 7% of your annual income on a set of golf clubs may not be logical to you, think about some of the emotional reasons your customers spend money.

To be better looking

To have thinner hips

To have larger breasts

To have more hair

To learn more

To smell better

To enjoy an expensive gourmet meal

To stay at an exotic vacation resort

To reduce stress

To impress a girlfriend/boyfriend with a gift

To raise their social status

To overcome depression

To enhance their hobby

To feel smarter

Want to hear something really scandalous?

I heard a sales manager at a big warehouse food outlet argue with me about the distinction between luxury items and commodities. He said,

> *"That doesn't apply to us, we aren't in the luxury business. We just give people the lowest price on every day items. Emotion doesn't apply to commodities; commodities being staples like toothpaste, milk, canned vegetables and the like. People have to buy this stuff and they want to*

get the lowest 'club' price. We can't create a
relationship over an end cap item like aspirin."

Hmm, maybe he should try telling that to the Bayer aspirin people. I'm sure the aspirin folks have case studies to show that a customer with a splitting headache is in a highly emotional state. Maybe that customer isn't as concerned about getting the 'club price' as they are trying to recover from a throbbing skull and blurred eyesight?

I left thinking that this guy had better buy the *Chicken Soup for the Unemployed Soul* book. Or, stock up on aspirin…because he's going to have one whale of a headache when he realizes how wrong he's been.

NOW, WE KNOW SCIENTIFICALLY…
IF CUSTOMERS LIKE YOU
THEY WILL COME BACK.

The customer loyalty equation doesn't get more elementary than this. We return to people we like.

In High School Biology, we learned that our brains and neurological functions respond quickly and unconsciously to the extremes of pleasure and pain. Kahneman proved that our brains react to pleasure and pain during transactions in commerce, as well. We avoid those responses (transactions) that caused us pain. The pleasurable response, in commerce, means that we want to do more business with companies and people we find "likeable."

If customers like you, they will remember you; especially if the final memory is a pleasurable one. Kahneman gives an interesting example of a series of experiments with a dentist giving Novocain injections.

In the first test, the dentist inserted the needle, injected the pain killer and pulled the needle out immediately. The process took about 10 seconds. Patients complained; saying that his injections were very painful. In the second test, the same dentist repeated the same injection process but left the penetrated needle in the patient's mouth for ten seconds after the fluid had been injected. Then, he removed the needle. Patients characterized this dentist as very gentle and would like to go see him again. Even though the test patients had to endure the needle in their mouths for twice the amount of time, they actually left with a better memory. Kahneman cites this as another example of irrationality overriding logic. The final (positive) memory is the strongest factor for determining likeability and a repeat visit. So, even if you mess up the entire transaction, salvaging the final moment is the one your customers will remember most.

The importance of that final moment is consistent with how we react to our other memories.

In love, when you are kissing your spouse goodbye at the airport, in the event of an accident, you want to take that nice memory with you.

In show business, an entertainer always wants to leave you "wanting more."

The hype for any television series is always reserved for "the final episode."

Even in TV news, the station will always attempt to close the broadcast with a cute "kicker story." You know what I'm talking about. The news anchor will announce, *"We lost 60,000 people in the Tsunami, 20 soldiers were killed in Iraq today...but up next, we found a squirrel who can water ski!"*

Why do they do that?

Because they want you to like them enough to tune in tomorrow.

CUSTOMERS ALSO HAVE AN "ASSOCIATIVE MEMORY"

When a customer leaves you, they may have a subconscious feeling they aren't able to explain. Customers remember good times and will unconsciously keep going back to the same man, woman, business, or product hoping to repeat the experience.

Malcolm Gladwell, in *Blink,* described how a soft drink manufacturer was surprised to learn that customers not only made decisions on the taste and the store experience, but also relative to the associative environment in which they were drinking the soft drink. For example, if the drink was served at a party with friends and family—and the party was a rousing success—the customer would unconsciously repurchase that same brand for the next party.

You've seen it.

In the last ten years, beverage manufacturers try to create that associative experience (prior to the purchase) by showing people having a good time or being successful with a gorgeous member of the opposite sex.

Malcolm and I were on a speaking engagement together and I asked him if opposite associative memory triggers could be true. What if your advertising sets up an expectation that your product can't deliver? How could that disappointment affect the associative experience? I'm paraphrasing here but Malcolm essentially told me, *"Over-promising can have a profoundly negative effect on the experience. The anticipation—accompanied by subsequent disappointment—could actually have a dis-associative effect—in other words, a subconscious avoidance response."*

Wow! We don't want our customers to avoid us—consciously or unconsciously. Be really careful about over-promising.

EMOTIONS RULE!

Anytime you separate hard earned cash from the tight folds of a customer's wallet, the decision is *always* emotionally based. That's why an emotional connection with your customer is so vitally important.

So, don't waste your time arguing with another person's "logic" because it may never seem logical to you.

CHAPTER 10

BIG CHANGE #6
DON'T SETTLE FOR A BUSINESS RELATIONSHIP

Customers don't want a business relationship with you. They want a friendship.

"Relationship building" is probably the most popular topic discussed at every annual corporate convention.

Whenever I go over the content checklist of my speeches, invariably the client will say, "Can you be sure to stress *relationship building*?" Organizations know relationships are important to generating customers and profits but may still be unsure how to pull it off.

CUSTOMERS ONLY HAVE ONE RELATIONSHIP BAROMETER

Because we are all subject to the laws of human nature, your customers use the same barometer to measure their personal relationships as they do their business relationships.

Think about why your own personal relationships endure. It doesn't matter if it is an old friend or a romantic interest...you have a long term relationship with someone because you like that person. You want to spend time with that person. You like to hear their voice on the phone. You confide in and trust that person. That person listens when you talk and can empathize with your troubles. If you haven't seen that person in a long time, you can't wait to "catch up."

And, why do some of those relationships wither and die?

Maybe that person lied to you, betrayed you, humiliated you, was constantly "negative"...or worse...that person neglected you.

When we feel continually rejected or neglected by a friend, the good feelings we once felt start to dissipate.

People describe the death of a relationship in painful ways. "I couldn't stand being around that much negative energy"—"We outgrew each other"—"He still wanted to act like we were in High School"—"She was always bringing me down"—"He was a control freak"—"It was always about HER."

Those emotional descriptors wear us down and we'll eventually stop seeing that person.

WOMEN KNOW THIS ALREADY

The fact that women are better at building and retaining relationships should come as no surprise to you.

They invented the art.

And when it comes to business, their human interactive skills clearly outperform us men.

The *Center for Women's Business Research* reported that since 1997, in female owned and operated businesses, hiring employees was up 18%, revenues were up 32%, and number of companies started was up 11%. Pretty impressive considering that happened during a time in our history when the dot.com implosion crushed so many companies and left tens of thousands of employees without work.

How were they able to do that?

Relationships.

Seems that women are more savvy than we men at knowing how to thrive during an economic downturn.

I used to joke in my nightclub act that, "Women study relationships so intently that they take a quiz every month in their magazines. In our magazines, we don't even have words."

But it's true, isn't it?

Women communicate more often (and better) than men.

According to Faith Popcorn in her book, *EVEolution; The 8 Truths of Marketing to Women,* if a woman likes a product or service, she will recommend (it) to an average of 21 other people. If a man likes a product or service he will only recommend (it) to 2.6 other people.

Judy B. Rosener in her book, *America's Competitive Secret: Women Managers,* has a lot of insight on how women think.

> *"Women link [rather than rank] workers; favor*
> *interactive-collaborative leadership style*
> *[empowerment beats top-down decision making];*
> *sustain fruitful collaborations; comfortable with*
> *sharing information; see redistribution of power*
> *as victory, not surrender; favor multi-dimensional*

feedback; value technical & interpersonal skills,
individual & group contributions equally; readily
accept ambiguity; honor intuition as well as pure
"rationality"; inherently flexible; appreciate
cultural diversity."

Beyond their obvious empathy and interpersonal skills, women seem to be able to create and sustain relationships for biological reasons.

At a neurological conference, I heard a brain doctor claim that a woman's brain can fire synapses (3) times faster than a man's brain. Because of that, there is strong evidence to suggest that women multi-task better than men. While men seem to be able to focus on one thing at a time, women can keep a lot of balls in the air. For men, when that one thing is a sales goal, there is little room in his brain to flip on the empathy switch.

DO WOMEN REALLY HAVE INTUITION?

Women are far better at reading faces and interpreting words than most of the men I know.

But I don't think it's intuition.

Women use a far more devious trick.

They listen.

Because they are generally better listeners, women are tuned in to hear the *meaning* behind the words. If a man senses a woman is upset, he may say, "Are you OK?" If the woman utters a quivering response like, "Oh, I'm fiiinnne," the man walks away thinking he's been adequately sensitive by asking the question, and she said she was fine. However, a woman would hear that and start to probe; knowing the quiver in her voice meant she *wasn't* fine. A woman compares the audible information with the saddened face, and a whole other conversation is hatched.

If our man in question had been practiced to notice a saddened or frustrated facial expression—combined with a quivering voice, he would have responded in a completely different, more empathetic way. Instead, he came off as an uncaring and uninterested jerk.

TAKE A BOLD STEP

So, how do you start to build a relationship with your customers?

Ask questions.

Show interest in them.

Learn as much as you can about that person and allow them to get to know you.

From our research, we know that,

(1) Many customers are feeling vulnerable, powerless, defenseless, out of control, or uncomfortable and...

(2) They already expect customer service to be horrible, so they're on guard for a possible confrontation.

Given those emotions, the fastest way to connect with a new friend is to show immediate empathy. Making an effort to "be understanding" automatically endears people to you.

FYI: PSYCHOGRAPHICS AREN'T RELATIONSHIP BUILDERS

A lot has been made about the value of psychographics as a tool to knowing your customers. They're fine to use for supplementary information, but don't mistake exhaustive psychographic research as a substitute for building a "relationship." It's historic data; not a relationship.

Knowing what people buy, what they do in their spare time, how many children they have, and what beer they drink is only a voyeuristic view of your customer's past behaviors.

But instead of trying to extrapolate a link between their hobbies and habits—to your products and services, why not get up close, look them in the eye and ask them how you can be a part of their lives?

Better yet, behave in such a way that *they* want to create a relationship with *you*.

CHAPTER 11

BIG CHANGE #7
FALL IN LOVE WITH YOUR CUSTOMERS

Love is the essential element you'll need if you want to earn loyal customers because...

CUSTOMERS WANT TO BE LOVED

Please don't think I am suggesting you manipulate your customers into an emotionally loyal state.

But I am suggesting that we are all human beings who need to be loved.

You have to believe that your customers want to be loved and respected. They can't help it. It's a primal human need.

Again, think of it in terms of your personal relationships.

Getting married is the final and most committed step in a love relationship. The emotional commitment is so strong that you promise to love, honor, cherish, and remain faithful to one person for the rest of your life.

That kind of loyalty would be the dream of every business owner.

Long term loyalty is achievable but it's critical to remember that *all* of the steps of the "courtship" have to be strictly followed, in the following order.

Initial Attraction
(marketing message)

+

Building Trust
(keeping promises)

+

Handling Difficulties Well
(complaints & disputes)

+

Creating an Emotional Bond
(cementing a strong relationship)

=

Long Term Loyalty through Ongoing Trust & Love

Loyalty in marriage and in a business relationship only sustains when there is a strong *emotional connection* to keep both of you there. "Getting what you need out of the relationship; emotionally," as psychotherapists so often repeat.

Allow me to give you an incentive to love your customers.

Money. Lots and lots of money.

Emotional loyalty yields enormous profits.

Frederick F. Reichheld writes in his book, *The Loyalty Effect,*

> *"The effect of turning even a small proportion of ordinary customers into loyal customers leads to an average increase in profit-per-customer of more than 25%."*

You want job security?
Generate emotionally loyal customers.

You want a raise in salary?
Generate emotionally loyal customers.

You want to increase your stock price?
Generate emotionally loyal customers.

People who can develop emotionally loyal customers allow you to grow your division, your business, or your market share—from within (organically)—*without* spending additional advertising money. In fact, emotionally loyal customers are the most important extension of your marketing department.

Loyal followers refer the best qualified new customers to you.

If you have a problem, emotionally loyal customers are more likely to handle a "bump in the road" more graciously than a customer farther down in the courtship process.

Emotionally loyal customers will pay more for services and goods—because they would rather do business with you than risk their money with someone they don't' know.

LOYALTY MEANS LESS HEADACHES

Jim Clifton, CEO of the Gallup Organization, told a small group of us that he was approached by a rival phone company with an offer to cut the Gallup phone bill by $500,000. When you're a company whose livelihood depends on telephone surveys, a savings of a half million dollars gets your attention. So, Jim went to his telephone department to see if the switch made sense. The phone services manager said, *"I think we should stay with (current phone company). We have a good relationship and if there is a problem we know they will take care of it. I just don't think we should risk using another service."*

Jim didn't make the switch...not even for half a million dollars!

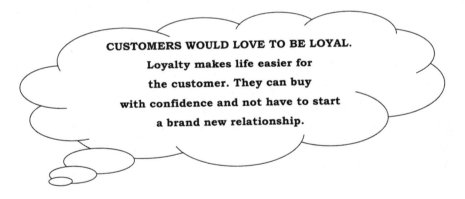

CUSTOMERS WOULD LOVE TO BE LOYAL.
Loyalty makes life easier for
the customer. They can buy
with confidence and not have to start
a brand new relationship.

JOHN HIXON MEETS STANLEY MARCUS

One of the best success stories I've heard about "loving your customers" came from John Hixon of Sweetwater, Texas.

Twenty years ago, James inherited his father's grocery store. Sounded like a nice "gift" until John learned that the store was hemorrhaging gobs of cash every day. John was doing about $250,000 in annual sales but losing $200,000 of it. An accountant told Hixon that he needed to either create a brand new business or try to copy a successful one. Hixon said he had always admired Stanley Marcus (of Neiman Marcus fame). The accountant said, *"Fine. I'm going to refund my fee. You go see Stanley Marcus in Dallas."*

Go see *the* Stanley Marcus? Hixon froze with fear.

Dallas was a huge city compared to Sweetwater. And Stanley Marcus was a worldwide legend. John was convinced that Mr. Marcus wouldn't take a meeting with a small town grocer. The consultant just said, *"How do you know unless you call him?"* It took Hixon several weeks to get up the courage to call Marcus' office. When he finally reached Marcus' secretary, she said, *"I'm sorry. Mr. Marcus can't see you today."*

Hixon was actually relieved that his instincts had been right... until the woman said, *"But he can see you tomorrow at 2 p.m."*

With his heart pounding, he ventured into The Big "D" the next day. Stanley Marcus met a timid John Hixon with a firm handshake and a welcoming smile. *"What can I do for you son?"* Marcus said. Hixon explained that his store was losing a lot of money and he didn't know why. Marcus said, *"Sweetwater, huh? Let me ask you something. Do you love your customers?"* Hixon said, *"Sure."* Then Marcus said, *"Great. Here's a piece of paper. Write down your 50 best customers. Write down their names and the names of their spouses and children."*

Hixon stared at the paper and, after six long minutes, was only able to fill in four names.

Marcus looked at him and said, *"Son, you don't love your customers. Go back to your store and love them. Stand by the door when they come in and tell them you're glad they* came in. *If they can't find an item, don't point them down an aisle. Walk them over to the olive or the raisins. Then, be there when they walk out and tell them you want to see them again. Tell them how much you and your family appreciate their business. Then, come back next year and tell me how it worked out."*

Hixon told me he was thrilled to be able to go back to Dallas, just nine months later, and tell Stanley Marcus that he had followed through—and that his little store had grossed $1.5 million in sales!

CHAPTER 12

BIG CHANGE #8
CREATE A
CUSTOMER
COMMUNITY

So how can you get customers to *stay* in love with you?

By giving them an ongoing place in your life. Customers want you to create a "community" for them.

Even though the suburbanization of America has caused communities to splinter and disengage, human nature's need to get together still burns hot. All of us, in business, need to be aware of how communities operate, what they want, and what opportunities exist within those communities.

It starts with accepting this premise:

Humans are pack animals. We need other people. We want to be in a community with others.

CREATE YOUR OWN "COMPANY COMMUNITY"

You can create your own corporate community.

You can create your own brand "club."

Design and sell cool looking hats or shirts that bear your logo. (Go to a Harley Davidson store and check out the motor clothes department for ideas)

Create a newsletter with valuable "content" other than just your latest sale items. Costco Wholesale has a magazine called *The Costco Connection* that features articles germane to small business owners.

Stage interesting (& free) monthly or bi-monthly events at your location. It could be a fashion show, a car rally, a celebrity autograph signing, a contest, a food tasting fair, a battle-of-the-bands, an exhibition of unusual items, a high school fundraiser, a temporary museum, face painting, a "new artists" music concert, pet fair, costume day, or anything else that doesn't necessarily orbit around an obvious excuse to push merchandise.

In other words, do something for your community; something that is in *their* best interest; not yours. Trust me on this. Your customers will remember who staged the event.

TIE *YOUR* BUSINESS INTO OTHER "COMMUNITIES"

There are dozens of other ways to connect your community to existing communities. Here are a few you may not have thought of yet.

THE INTERNET COMMUNITIES; CHATS, BLOGS, & PODS

People are so desperate to connect with a community of other like-minded people that you can find literally millions of Internet Chat Rooms on every possible interest; legal and illegal. Chat Rooms have sub-groups that cater to specific kinds of chat—called News Groups.

Blogs are the latest social craze to explode geometrically.

Blogs are open comment sites about every possible subject. Anyone who knows how to find a Blog can participate in a Blog page.

According to www.whatis.techtarget.com, the definition of a blog is:

> "a blog (short for _weblog_) is a personal journal
> that is frequently updated and intended for
> general public consumption. Blogs generally
> represent the personality of the author or reflect
> the purpose of the Web site that hosts the blog.
> Topics sometimes include brief philosophical
> musings, commentary on Internet and other
> social issues, and links to other sites the author
> favors. The essential characteristics of the blog
> are its journal form, typically a new entry each
> day, and its informal style.

To start a Blog you only need a computer and in Internet connection.

Then, you go to a site like www.livejournal.com or www.Blogger.com and you can set one up; for free. Microsoft is also in the Blog business at www.spaces.msn.com. Microsoft lets you create a simple blog with text, links, and photos. Or, just post your Blog on any number of sites that offer the ability for you to post your thoughts, opinions, editorials, whatever.

There is yet another Internet community about to take a leap from infancy to a full blown phenomenon.

Podcasting!

Podcasting, as you can imagine, takes its name from the Apple iPod.

Podcasting is a cool new form of micro-casting that could soon be as significant as cable TV.

The idea is this.

Use your computer to record an MP3 file. An MP3 file is a digital audio file of *you* talking about a compelling subject. Next, post that file somewhere on your web site. Finally, ask interested people to log onto that web site and download the MP3 program to their iPod or computer.

Bam! You're a broadcaster!

Yes, with a cheap microphone and a computer, you can actually record your own personal "radio show" and invite others to listen to it anywhere in the world.

One of the most listened to Podcasts is the *Dawn and Drew Show*. Dawn and Drew are a married couple who live in an old farmhouse outside Wayne, Wisconsin. Every night they do their "radio" show. It lasts about 30 minutes. They usually argue "on-air" but a lot of their "show" consists of funny, stupid, stream of consciousness blather. What's remarkable is that 9,000 downloads have occurred from their 70+ episodes. The Dawn & Drew community is growing!

You can hear them for yourself at www.dawnanddrew.com.

Music reviews are another Podcast favorite. Adam Curry, former MTV V-Jay does his Podcast from his home in London, England. Adam is largely thought to be the creator of this phenomenon with his show, *The Daily Source Code.* He covers the Podcasting phenomenon and can be found at www.dailysourcecode.com.

Other Podcasts cater to every micro interest you can imagine. From *Sup with Jesus* to *Yeast Radio*—a drag queen download.

The huge benefit for your Podcast audience is that they can download your program and listen whenever they want to. It's like having TIVO for your computer.

If you think you have something interesting to say, why not create a Podcast for your business. You don't need expensive broadcasting gear. You just need a computer, a cheap microphone, and free software you can get at www.podcastalley.com.

Will Podcasts catch on? My guess is a resounding yes!

Nobody thought Blogs would be popular—but even old school companies like General Motors have Blog sites. A ChevyPodcast can't be far behind.

THE VIDEO GAME COMMUNITY

You can infiltrate the video game community.

More than 42 million American households own a video gaming console such as PlayStation 2 or X-Box. And they aren't just being played by the family.

Video Game aficionados are now able to log on and play games (to wage video war) against virtually thousands of other players all around the globe.

That's a community!

Video games like *Halo, Call of Duty, Counterstrike*, and *Warcraft III* have worldwide tournaments and rankings.

Hollywood has realized that a successful game associated with a movie can sometimes out-gross the ticket revenue of the original movie. They also know that buying the movie rights to a popular video game can bring an enormous pre-sold audience to the movie theater. Movie, sports, and music stars clamor to be "cast" in a new game because; (1) they know it speaks to a valuable younger audience, and (2) there are huge dollars involved. Stars can bank from $50,000 to a million bucks lending their name and character to a highly anticipated new title.

Of particular interest to your business is the fact that this community has purchased millions of copies of these games. And, game buyers all recommend other "hot" games to each other. Tap into this community (through product placement) and you've got an overnight audience in the millions.

THE MOTOR COMMUNITIES

Maybe you've got something that will appeal to the thousands of car club enthusiasts? If so, combine your community with theirs.

When urban communities broke into suburbs and we became a commuter culture, driving a car to work became a necessity. Our cars soon reflected who we were and how much money we had. Cars became extensions of our personalities and we identified with others who bought our brand. The car club was born.

Worldwide variations of "Hot Rod" clubs have been around since the late 40's. Ferrari has a passionate group called *The Prancing Horses*. Porsche has an owners group called *POC* (Porsche Owners Club)

All you have to do is channel surf and you'll see the overcrowded "motor shows" on the Discovery Channel, MTV, Spike TV, and others. People love vehicles so much that they will sit down, for hours, and watch them being assembled.

I'm not immune, myself.

As a life long motorcycle rider, last year I bought a Harley Davidson *Road King.*

I was instantly absorbed into *that* community!

Seriously, Harley Davidson does a wonderful job of creating a community within that brand. When you buy a new motorcycle, the company sends you a videotape titled, *Welcome to the Family.* They also send you a one year membership in H.O.G. (*Harley Owners Group*) which includes discounts on bike rentals when you visit another city, a monthly magazine, membership pins, and maps of "great rides." Membership in H.O.G. now tops 900,000 members worldwide.

How passionate are the fans about this brand? Some tattoo the Harley logo on their bodies. Others will place Harley logos in the form of decals and bumper stickers on their cars, trucks and trailers.

So, how do you integrate your company into this community or one like it? Take a lesson from my friend, Frank Candy. Frank is the founder and President of American Speakers Bureau Corporation®. He is a successful business owner, speaker, author, and third generation Harley-Davidson® motorcycle rider who has attended all of the major motorcycle events around the country. Frank describes the experience like this;

> *"It's the evening of July 4th, 2005. The sun has set and the thunderclouds are building quickly. I just returned from a motorcycle rally in Plant City, Florida with over 12,000 motorcycle enthusiasts who enjoy the bike shows, the vendors, bars, restaurants, and live entertainment. This was a small one.*
>
> *Bike Week in Daytona Beach Florida drew over 550,000 people in 2005. The Rally in Sturgis, South Dakota (in August) is expected to draw at least that many.*
>
> *Having been involved with many charity fund raises all my life, (my parents were very big on community involvement and improvement) and because our family has been riding these bikes*

for three generations, H.O.G. (The Harley Owners Group®) had a unique appeal for me. As a group, they offer the opportunity to connect with other people who enjoy the sport. But on a deeper level they are some of the most generous people I have ever met.

Based on these facts I volunteered to be the Director Of Public Relations for the Seminole County Harley Owners Group® of Central Florida. My role is to interact with the media, request and collect items for our charity auctions, and promote our events. As a professional speaker for over 20 years, I am not bashful, so this was an easy role for me to fulfill.

Most all of these rides are well organized and almost all of them support a good charity that needs help and money. It's usually for the sick and unfortunate, or animals and the ones closest to my heart, the veterans. Over the years I have seen more than a few tears sliding from under sunglasses. Everyone gets affected, even the most grizzled, well-traveled bikers.

With all this opportunity to give back to the community, I also had what Ross calls the "spin off for business opportunity". Beside motorcycles, my interests in charities, racing, golf, boating, aeronautics and the Internet have opened many doors for outstanding friendships and business relationships with great people."

To galvanize this community point, I ask my audiences if anyone else rides a Harley. A few hands always go up. We don't know each other but a couple of Harley riders who have never met, can talk for 90 minutes about each other's bike.

"Did you chrome the hand controls?"

"What exhaust are you running?"

"Did you notice a performance improvement with the Stage I Kit?"

Harley owners (worldwide) even have a secret hand signal we use with other Harley riders on the road. There is a sticky bond between riders of these motorcycles that transcends continents and language. It's a love affair with the brand. It's a kind of mutual respect and sense of "community" that metric bike owners (Honda, Kawasaki, Suzuki, and Yamaha) don't understand.

Harley Davidson also has a "motor clothes" division that sells so well that Harley Davidson couldn't possibly match the exposure with TV and radio advertising. Millions of fans unabashedly wear the Harley logo on T-shirts, leather jackets, headbands, gloves, vests, and even thong underwear. And that isn't even counting the Harley Davidson pet clothing line!

CLOTHING COMMUNITIES DO IT

Harley Davidson's clothing success doesn't surprise other clothing designers. Clothes have always been a self generating "community."

You should have a clothing line. They are mobile billboards for your brand.

Ask any fashion forward man or woman about clothing brand awareness and you'll get an earful about how certain brands become a community all their own. I've seen other women spot my wife's handbag and there is an instant eye-contact-bond of recognition. I had no idea there was a purse community.

Is anyone old enough to remember *Members Only* jackets? If you wore one you were in a club that had no clubhouse, no meetings, and no purpose.

Look at the success Sean Combs (P. Diddy) has had with his *Sean John* clothing line.

Russell Simmons and his *Phat Farm* brand.

Vans shoes to the skateboard community.

And who can deny the popularity of the *Major League Baseball, National Football League,* and the *National Basketball Association* signature clothing. Wear the clothes and you're associated with the club.

Clothing brands become communities by virtue of label acceptance and your participation.

THE NEW CHURCH COMMUNITY

What Rick Warren of *Saddleback Church* does so expertly is that he encourages his attendees (80,000+) to form communities he calls "small groups" (4–12 people). He wants small groups to meet once a week, on their own, outside of church. These groups aren't like the old Bible Study clubs—but rather an opportunity to connect with people in your neighborhood. The small groups act as a support system for each other. Often, these groups work together to help out needy families or community causes. Some of the groups have become such good friends they go on vacation together.

The small group concept has had a sweeping global effect. There are literally tens of thousands of churches who now subscribe to the Saddleback model.

HOUSING COMMUNITIES ARE GOING BACK TO THE FUTURE

Even communities are trying to be communities again.

Look at the best selling housing developments like *Ladera Ranch* in Mission Viejo, California, *The Grove* in Los Angeles, and *Blackhawk* in San Ramon. These housing developments are being built to replicate a small town-within-a-city. If you buy a condo or detached home in these areas, you are within walking distance to the post office, the grocery store, the dry cleaner, several restaurants, schools, parks, churches, and more. There is often a waiting list to buy homes in these communities because people want to live *a connected life.*

The Walt Disney Co. was one of the first companies to recognize there was a demand for a retro home town. Disney built the community of *Celebration;* near Kissimmee, Florida.

Celebration looks like a town from a 1940's or 1950's Disney movie. The architecture of the homes, shops, schools, medical facilities, restaurants, and the post office are reminiscent of a happier era. And, families will pay handsomely for this experience. When my wife and I were there, only two homes were for sale; a 3,200 square foot home selling for $670,000...and a 4,200 square foot home for just under one million dollars.

Old Yeller not included.

BE POLITICALLY ACTIVE IN YOUR COMMUNITY

Every one of us should be a member of at least three local organizations who serve our community. The exposure alone extends your reach and influence geometrically.

The math is simple.

If you take an interest in your community, they will take an interest in you.

We did something altruistic for our "television" community and they rewarded us with their unconditional loyalty.

In the late 80's, I was hosting a local TV show in Seattle, Washington called *Almost Live.* It had been a few really sad years for Washington state politics. Plus, the state had been hit hard due to an announcement that the Boeing Aircraft Company was moving their headquarters out of town. So, several of us came up with an idea to involve our community in a fun "community action" event.

Something to distract our community from all the bad news.

We proposed changing the official song of Washington State to the 60's rock hit, *Louie, Louie.*

Here's what happened.

Washington State already had a state song titled, *Washington My Home,* but nobody knew it existed. We thought this was the perfect (and harmless) law worth changing. We passed out *Louie, Louie* buttons and I went to the state capitol in Olympia to plead with the state legislators.

Unwittingly, we'd hit a much bigger nerve than we ever could have anticipated.

The groundswell of public support for this silly idea was staggering. 5,000 people showed up, during a workday, to support *Louie, Louie* for the state song. *Paul Revere and the Raiders* flew in to play the song. So did *The Kingsmen* (who recorded the version most people remember) and *The Wailers.* Two High School orchestral bands. Oh, and so did everyone in the news media.

We were instantly famous.

In some form or another, the *Louie, Louie* campaign was in the press for 261 straight days. We even won the Dubious Achievement Award from *Esquire Magazine.*

A full-on bona fide phenomenon was taking place.

Everywhere I went people wanted to know about the campaign. Even Dick Clark and Ed McMahon invited me on their national *Bloopers and Practical Jokes* show to talk about the Capitol rally. It was huge!

With one major snag.

The original author of *"Washington My Home"* was still alive...and she was really ticked off.

Helen Davis, 86, lived in Pasco, Washington got involved in the melee. What did she think of these upstart TV boys who threatened to unseat her song? She demanded equal broadcast time. She went on a Spokane radio station and said, *"If that Ross Shafer wants to change the state song to Louie, Louie, he might as well change the state flower to marijuana."*

Harsh words.

I went on TV the next week and said, *"Look Helen, one campaign at a time. We are totally swamped with the song thing."*

I CAN'T EMPHASIZE THIS ENOUGH

As human beings, we all need and want a sense of community; where we live and where we shop. A community, of any kind, connects us to other people. Provide a community for your customers and you'll help cement their love for you.

CHAPTER 13

BIG CHANGE #9
SCRAP YOUR CURRENT CUSTOMER ''EVALUATIONS''

SURVEYS AREN'T GIVING YOU
WHAT YOU NEED

Customers told us they are *never* in the mood to take another test, fill out a form, or discuss the "experience," at *your* convenience.

Our research told us that if customers had a really rotten experience they would say something. If their experience was spectacular, they also might speak up—but better yet—they would tell other people.

But what about the silent masses who say nothing? Some organizations replicate insecure teenage boy behavior then they constantly worry, *"She didn't say call me back. Does she like me? Maybe she hates me? What did I do wrong? I will be whoever she wants me to be if she will just tell me what she wants."*

I'm urging you to consider that surveys, telephone calls, evaluation forms, and any other customer review devices only circumnavigate listening to the customer's face-to-face feedback.

Rick Barerra, in his runaway best selling book, *Overpromise and Overdeliver,* tells the story of Feargal Quinn, the owner of nineteen supermarkets in Ireland. The Superquinn stores are extraordinarily successful because Quinn is a hands-on owner who is passionate about customer service. Barerra says, (Quinn) *"...is particularly adamant about one thing: Don't depend on market research or a suggestion box. Talk to customers and actively seek out their complaints."*

From what we heard, evaluation forms are worthless; not to mention exhausting, time consuming, potentially humiliating, and arguably the single most irritating item designed to ruin the rest of the buying experience.

Here's why.

First of all, each form is laid out differently. The form makes the customer feel stupid because it takes time for them to deduce how they feel about service; using *your* measurement terms.

On a scale of 1–10, Is the food a 5? Is the cleanliness a 7? What if my 7 is someone else's 4? Will my 7 cancel out someone else's 3? Am I "More Likely" to come back? Or, am I "Least Likely" to tell other people?

You're asking too much from the customer; post mortem.

Management loves written evaluations because they think they can make decisions about people and procedures based on collected data. Management also thinks they can design the questions to monitor how well their "plan" is being executed.

But it's a flawed measurement.

Humans don't have perfect memories. And their scores are colored by their mood, at that moment. Customers may be marking down all high scores because you are bribing them with a discount off their next meal—or offering them a prize of some kind. I even heard that Target Stores was offering a chance to win $20,000 if you participated in their phone survey.

On the following pages are a few of the evaluation forms I've seen. Ask yourself if you would be "in the mood" to fill them out completely and accurately.

Purchase/Lease Survey

• Please use pencil or blue or black ink to fill in the box with an X.   Example: ☒

Our records show you purchased/leased your

Do you own/lease this vehicle? ☐ Yes (Continue) ☐ No ☐ Never owned (if you marked 'no' or 'never owned', please return survey in envelope provided)

Did you purchase/lease at this dealership? ☐ Yes (Continue) ☐ No (Please return survey in envelope provided) 0412241006482

Product presentation

1 Please rate your **SALESPERSON** on each of the following:

	Excellent	Good	Average	Fair	Poor	Not Applicable
Prompt initial greeting	☐	☐	☐	☐	☐	
Courtesy/friendliness	☐	☐	☐	☐	☐	
Integrity	☐	☐	☐	☐	☐	
Matched vehicle to your needs	☐	☐	☐	☐	☐	
Considerate of your time	☐	☐	☐	☐	☐	
Ability to answer your questions	☐	☐	☐	☐	☐	
Test drive	☐	☐	☐	☐	☐	☐
Knowledge of models/features	☐	☐	☐	☐	☐	

Comments on question 1:

Negotiation

2 During your price/payment **NEGOTIATION** experience, how would you rate the following?

	Excellent	Good	Average	Fair	Poor
Simple and straightforward	☐	☐	☐	☐	☐
Honesty	☐	☐	☐	☐	☐
Your comfort with the process	☐	☐	☐	☐	☐
Consideration for your time	☐	☐	☐	☐	☐
Knowledge of purchase/finance options	☐	☐	☐	☐	☐

Comments on question 2:

Final paperwork

3 Thinking about the **PERSON WHO COMPLETED YOUR FINAL PAPERWORK** (financing/leasing, registration, insurance, service contracts) how would you rate the following?

	Excellent	Good	Average	Fair	Poor
Concern for your needs	☐	☐	☐	☐	☐
Courtesy/friendliness	☐	☐	☐	☐	☐
Integrity	☐	☐	☐	☐	☐
Knowledge of products/services offered	☐	☐	☐	☐	☐
Explanation of documents/paperwork	☐	☐	☐	☐	☐
Ability to answer your questions	☐	☐	☐	☐	☐
Consideration for your time	☐	☐	☐	☐	☐
Accurately completed your paperwork	☐	☐	☐	☐	☐
Fulfilled negotiated commitments	☐	☐	☐	☐	☐

Comments on question 3:

Receiving your vehicle

4 When you picked up your new Toyota (**VEHICLE DELIVERY**), how would you rate the following?

	Excellent	Good	Average	Fair	Poor	Not Applicable
Provided all accessories as promised	☐	☐	☐	☐	☐	☐
Explanation of features/controls	☐	☐	☐	☐	☐	
Explanation of maintenance schedule and warranty	☐	☐	☐	☐	☐	
Ability to answer your questions	☐	☐	☐	☐	☐	
Consideration for your time	☐	☐	☐	☐	☐	
Expressed appreciation for your business	☐	☐	☐	☐	☐	

Comments on question 4:

This was only the 1st of the 4 pages I was asked to fill out when I bought my last car. They were asking me to recall every single detail of the transaction; even the negotiation process. Were the negotiations Excellent? Good? Fair? Poor? How should I know? I don't buy a car every day. I think the negotiation turned out good for *them*. Is there a line for that?

Some of the questions were just plain dumb. Did the vehicle match my needs? I wrote down. *"Not really. I have a bad habit of spending a lot of money on cars I can't use."*

I gave up and quit writing by page two.

What's wrong with this "high end" hotel evaluation?

If you would like to be contacted b regarding your comments, please in information:

Name _____

Street _____ Apt.#_____

City _____

State _____ Province _____

Country _____ Zip _____

Telephone # _____

Email _____

Dates of Stay: From _____ To _____

Room No.: _____

Please rate your satisfaction with each of the following:

	VERY SATISFIED	SOMEWHAT SATISFIED	NEUTRAL	SOMEWHAT DISSATISFIED	VERY DISSATISFIED
Overall satisfaction with this experience	☐	☐	☐	☐	☐
Receiving a warm and sincere greeting upon arrival	☐	☐	☐	☐	☐
Staff greeting you by name	☐	☐	☐	☐	☐
Staff remembering you as a regular guest	☐	☐	☐	☐	☐
Timeliness of check-in	☐	☐	☐	☐	☐
Receiving the room you expected	☐	☐	☐	☐	☐
Ability of the staff to anticipate your needs	☐	☐	☐	☐	☐
Cleanliness of the guest room	☐	☐	☐	☐	☐
Condition of the guest room furnishings	☐	☐	☐	☐	☐
Cleanliness of the hotel	☐	☐	☐	☐	☐
Condition of the hotel furnishings	☐	☐	☐	☐	☐
Quality of the food	☐	☐	☐	☐	☐
Receiving a fond farewell when you checked out	☐	☐	☐	☐	☐

VERY LIKELY SOMEWHAT LIKELY NEUTRAL SOMEWHAT UNLIKELY VERY UNLIKELY
☐ ☐ ☐ ☐ ☐
ely ☐ ☐ ☐ ☐ ☐

Did you experience any problems during your stay?
☐ Yes   ☐ No

If you reported any problems, how satisfied are you with the resolution ☐ ☐ ☐ ☐ ☐

Comments:
_____
_____
_____
_____
_____
_____
_____
_____
_____

Please suggest any service, product or amenity you would like added, or please let us know which exceptional ladies and gentlemen have made your stay more memorable.
_____
_____
_____
_____

Hotel Code: 0037   5-6635C (06/04)

The questions on the form are innocent enough. But you have to constantly twist your head sideways to read the description of your satisfaction level. And, of course, you have to learn a different format than the one we completed in the car evaluation layout.

Now, I have to decide if I am *Very Satisfied, Somewhat Satisfied, Neutral, Somewhat Likely,* or *Very Unlikely* to return.

This next example is so simple, I almost liked it.

---

1. Was your room available by the check in time of 3pm?

   ☐YES   ☐NO

   If not 3pm, around what time? _____

2. How satisfied were you with the cleanliness of your room?

   ☐ Exceeds Expectations   ☐ Met Expectations
            ☐ Did Not Meet Expectations

   If we did not meet your expectations, please explain:

3. How satisfied were you with the air quality and temperature of your room?

   ☐ Exceeds Expectations   ☐ Met Expectations
            ☐ Did Not Meet Expectations

   If we did not meet your expectations, please explain:

4. How satisfied were you with the knowledge of our staff you encountered during your stay? (i.e., Front Desk, Concierge...)

   ☐ Exceeds Expectations   ☐ Met Expectations
            ☐ Did Not Meet Expectations

   If we did not meet your expectations, please explain:

I say "almost" because the next page of the form was very confusing. They assumed I had "gotten the hang" of their *Exceed, Met, Did Not Meet Expectations* "test." Take a look at all of those letters.

Please mark which of the following restaurants or lounges you visited during your stay, and let us know how we measured up.

E= Exceeds Expectations   *M= Met Expectations*
D= Did Not Meet Expectations

	Food Quality	Quality Service	Value for Price Paid
☐ bluezoo	E M D	E M D	E M D
☐ Shula's	E M D	E M D	E M D
☐ Palio	E M D	E M D	E M D
☐ Kimonos	E M D	E M D	E M D
☐ Guillivers	E M D	E M D	E M D
☐ Fresh	E M D	E M D	E M D
☐ Garden Grve	E M D	E M D	E M D
☐ Dolphin Ftn	E M D	E M D	E M D
☐ Cabana	E M D	E M D	E M D
☐ Splash	E M D	E M D	E M D
☐ Tubbies	E M D	E M D	E M D
☐ Dolphin Lobby Lounge	E M D	E M D	E M D
☐ Lobby Ct. Lounge	E M D	E M D	E M D
☐ Room Service	E M D	E M D	E M D

If we did not meet your expectations, please explain:

See what I mean? It reads like an eye test! The sheer volume of the letters is overwhelming I can't see how this company could possibly get a representative sampling of accurate answers.

Do you see another flaw in the survey process?

Customers aren't skilled at judging their experience the way *you* want it to be judged; which gives surveys another possible layer of miscommunication. Besides, the final moment of the transaction may not be over, yet. What if the customer was so upset with the service at "The Cabin" that the customer decided "Tubanai"—and every other restaurant—was going to pay for the miscue, as well?

And what makes management think one evaluation form is right for every outlet...in every community?

I had one hotel manager, in the southern United States, tell me, *"I use the forms because (the chain) tells me to but I don't put much stock in them. A lot of people are still pretty racist down here—so when we get complaints we don't know if it's related to service or skin color."*

SO, WHAT'S THE ALTERNATIVE?

At the very least, take the forms away from the customer.

Don't make the customer do all of your work for you.

Better yet, do what Fergal Quinn does and actually talk to the customer face to face. Or, listen carefully to the front line people who must suffer the customer complaints.

If you work in a hotel, install a direct complaint phone line in every room. Put a sign on it that says, "If you are unhappy in any way, please pick up this phone." When a customer calls, the line would automatically ring the front desk or a separate customer service person. Then you pleasantly answer, "Thank you for calling, Mr. Smith. What can we correct for you?" Then, you say. "When we checked in, Bob was rude to my wife."...or... "We just got back from the seafood restaurant and the portions were very small for the price." Now, whoever is manning the complaint line pleasantly responds, "I apologize. I will take care of the problem (or) I will make sure management hears about this immediately." Then, *that employee* fills out the evaluation form. It's fast. It's immediate. And, it's directly from the customer's mouth. The other benefit is that the customer isn't stewing about this problem for their entire stay.

You could also try tossing out the subtleties.

A Hilton hotel in Lisle/Naperville, Illinois has a big sign in their lobby asking guests for an immediate opportunity to fix any glitches. I liked its bold approach and the fact that I didn't have to fill out a form.

THE PERFECT "10"

It is our goal that your stay is perfect! If your visit with us is anything less than perfect, please let us know so that we may be able to correct the issue right away. Our goal is to be the Top Rated hotel in customer service in the entire Hilton family. Thank you very much for helping us achieve our goal.

Richard Brink—General Manager

Or, how about posting a prominent sign; with a toll free number for the customer to call if he/she wants to report something good or something bad. Can you handle the truth?

Have a Good or Bad Comment about Us? Please Call: 1-800-555-COMMENT

If you are any other kind of business, think about installing an old fashioned "complaint box." Don't call it a "suggestion box" or anything else that softens the blow to your ego. Put one box in plain view and install another one in the restroom—or some other semi-private place. Make it an elegant (important looking) little box with a blank pad of paper (name, address, phone number is optional) and a good pen—held by a strong cord so it won't run away. If anyone has a specific complaint they can write it down, as soon as it happens, and stuff it in the box. That way you won't be intimidating customers by presenting them with a slough of irrelevant questions.

If you absolutely can't get away from having an evaluation form around, fill them out yourself. Train your people to listen for complaints and to write them down. Tell them to write down exactly what customers say and hand them directly to the manager.

E-TAILING EVALUATIONS AREN'T RELIABLE.

If you are an E-tailer who sells stuff through your web site, don't extort your customers to get a good "rating."

Some people prefer to buy online because they know what they want and don't have to leave home to get it. They also don't have to subject themselves to a miserable face-to-face customer service experience.

These buyers determine the reliability of the company by the highest number of "stars" or "happy faces" (or other symbol) the company is awarded by previous buyers. (If you want to see what I'm talking about go to www.pricegrabber.com, www.bizrate.com, www.nettag.com, etc).

If you have ever bought a used book or videotape from a private seller through EBay or Amazon, or any number of smaller retailers online, you have probably noticed this "Customer Rating." Sometimes the ratings will be based on thousands of previous transactions. If the rating has 4–5 Stars, you expect to have a good experience. A good experience usually means they have the item in stock, it is in the condition as advertised, and they will ship it promptly.

But are the "ratings" accurate?

Maybe.

Maybe not.

Two weeks before Christmas, I ordered a hard-to-find videotape for my sons (*Condorman* starring Michael Crawford; pre-*Phantom of the Opera* fame). The tape didn't arrive in time to put it under the tree and I wasn't very happy. When the tape finally made it to my door, there was a fuchsia green note inside that read:

> *"Hi and thanks for purchasing this video. I will leave positive feedback for you and hope that you will do the same for me. Please contact me before leaving less than a "5" for feedback. We guarantee satisfaction."*

See what's happening here? Bribery. Sellers are trying to manipulate their rating, as in *"I will scratch your back if you scratch mine."* Shame on you sellers who attempt to manipulate the rating process. Stop trying to bully people. Let the customer decide if you are offering good service or not.

BEWARE OF FOCUS GROUPS

Focus groups have too much power and too little skill.

I don't like focus groups because they are inexpert, human lab rats; who cannot accurately communicate under pressure. Besides, focus groups are the lazy way out of listening to your actual customers.

It has been popular for companies to spend a great deal of money to conduct focus groups. For the uninitiated, focus groups are small groups of people (10–25) who are trapped in a room, asked to watch a commercial—or taste a product—or witness behaviors—and then answer questions posed by a professional question-asker called a moderator. But the conditions of using the product or service aren't organic. They are sequestered in an out-of-context room—experimenting—with other out-of-context people. The moderator can make one small reaction error and unwittingly invalidate the discussion. On top of that, there are always emerging personality dynamics; as one person assumes the loudmouth leader role; thereby influencing the others.

Still, some management teams see this as a vital tool to help them make decisions.

Let's be honest.

The true purpose of the focus group is to corroborate somebody's gut *emotional* feeling. Somebody in management wants to push an idea forward but doesn't want to risk sticking out their lonely neck. So they hire people they think are potential users—to offer their "unbiased opinions." If the idea flops, the manager can always censure the focus group and say, *"I don't know why the idea failed. The focus group told us they loved the product."*

I think focus groups are an expensive waste of time when it comes to judging a customer's response. If you are an experienced and savvy judge of what people like, you don't need a focus group to endorse your gut.

Have some faith in your own experienced instincts.

If you believe in an idea, then have the courage of your conviction to try it. If it fails, do something else.

Why am I so bitter about focus groups?

I've sat in on dozens of post-focus-group marketing meetings.

As a TV host, I've personally been in the crosshairs of "the focus" many times. You'd think I'd be more tolerant; in that 90% of the time, I've been favorably "reviewed."

I'm not happy because I still know they aren't accurate.

Here's how it works in the television business. When a TV network wants to present a new program, they shoot a test show called a "pilot." Then, they test every substantial element of the pilot with potential viewers. They test the set design, the graphic elements, the music, the dialogue, and the show's premise (Example: Two guys share an apartment and discover they were married to the same woman). The most tested items of scrutiny are the actors and hosts. Since TV viewers are supposed to "fall in love" with the actors, the audience reaction is critical. One day, I sat behind a focus group one-way mirror where the moderator was testing a female host candidate. He asked the group these questions:

> "Which term best describes her? Cute, pretty, or sexy?"
>
> "Do you like her hair that way?"
>
> "Do you like the sound of her voice? If not, please describe it."
>
> "How about her taller height compared to the other actors?"
>
> "Women, would you like to have her as your best friend?"
>
> "Men, would you like to sleep with her?"

Beside the obvious offensive nature of the questions, there were several flaws in the questions asked. The questions were a result of one female executive's gut feeling "concerns;" which were already biased. The focus group was being asked to evaluate hair and voice and height—components that may not have occurred to them in a real world likeability test. Sometimes we are attracted to people because of their personality, laugh, charisma, etc.; regardless of a hairstyle.

Would you like to be judged like that?

Generally, if the TV project test comes back, "Positive. Absolutely through the roof"—then the network may order anywhere from 2 to 13 episodes. If the project scores badly by test audiences, it is usually scrapped.

Here's the final and most important fatal flaw.

If you trust focus groups to be so smart, then it follows that by using their test data, *every* TV show that tested "through the roof" would become a hit series.

As you know, they don't.

The latest estimates show that only 10% of TV pilots ever see the light of the public cathode ray tube. Even less survive past the initial episode order.

Maybe you'll find *this* funny.

A friend of mine hosted a pilot show that got rave reviews from the critics. Test audiences loved it. Sadly, it is reputed to have the shortest run of any TV show in history. The episode ran on a major network at 9:00pm eastern time...and was cancelled before the west coast airing (feed) of the show.

Test audiences really got this next example wrong.

In 1970, the ABC network tested the TV show *All in the Family*. More than 300 people watched the pilot and filled out survey cards. Test audiences didn't like it. So, ABC backed out. CBS picked it up and did their own round of testing. The results clearly stated that Archie Bunker was too mean and uncaring. Fortunately, programming director, Fred Silverman, liked the show and put it on anyway. On January 12, 1971, (as a mid-season replacement) *All in the Family* hit the airwaves and stayed in the top 20 for nine seasons.

Remember the famous Coke–Pepsi battle?

It was downright "guerilla" focus group testing.

In 1975, Pepsi took their film cameras into the streets and offered people a chance to compare Pepsi with Coke in a side-by-side taste test. Surprisingly, over 55% loved Pepsi. The campaign made marketing history and by 1976 Pepsi-Cola had convinced millions of soft drink buyers to switch; becoming the single largest-selling soft drink brand in America.

Coke panicked.

Then, they went into denial; doing nothing about their declining market share, for five years.

But in the early 80's they concluded that American taste buds had somehow changed and that they needed to create a brand new product. So, after exhaustive lab work, they invented a sweeter tasting (more Pepsi-like) formula and dubbed it, "New Coke."

Boldly, they ventured into scary marketing territory...and guess what?

The man-on-the-street-focus groups loved it!

Coke had taken it slow, done their homework, and their clever reinvention would surely spell doom for Pepsi.

By 1984, *New Coke* hit the grocery store shelves...and went into a coma.

It was an enormous flop.

New Coke was such a disaster that the company had to drop the new brand and bring back the original recipe; as *Classic Coke*. Something magical happened. Coke soon took over the lead again...and has held onto it ever since.

How can we explain this?

If Coke was initially the preferred brand, then why was Pepsi able to take the lead and cause enough panic for the Coke folks to change their winning formula? Did Pepsi cheat on the results?

Nope.

Taste experts say it's because Pepsi's first splash to the mouth hits the taste buds as a bit "sweeter" than Coke. So, in a small "swig" taste test, Pepsi would win. Back that up with a cosmic-sized media campaign that shows people having a pleasantly surprised, enthusiastic reaction, and you can move a lot of people to switch brands.

But it didn't last.

Customers switched back to coke. It turns out that if you drink a whole can of Pepsi, the sweet taste becomes too sweet. Coke is a better tasting "full can" drink than a "swig."

Focus groups can even fool themselves...for a while.

INSTEAD, HIRE TRAINED INVESTIGATORS

I love the mystery/secret shopper concept.

They are the best private investigators money can buy.

Secret shopping doesn't require any effort from the customer and, if done correctly, it provides you with the most honest and direct feedback to the company. The best feature of secret shopping is that it fills in the blanks; i.e., the feedback missing from surveys.

Judith Hess, owner of *Customer Perspectives* in Hooksett, New Hampshire, told me,

"Most (solicited) surveys are filled out by people who really like the place or really hate the place. The secret shopper represents the silent majority, the customer in the middle, who never says anything and never fills out those things."

If you aren't aware of how the secret shopping process works, here's a short primer. Company XYZ hires a mystery shopping company and gives their "shoppers" real money to pretend to be real shoppers. The amount of spending money, per transaction, can be from $5 on up; depending on the price of the items being shopped. The shoppers are carefully trained to absorb everything about the shopping experience. Company XYZ has designed a report form; which the shopper then fills out as a transaction "post mortem." The report may have questions like:

Was the employee friendly?

Was he/she attractively dressed?

Was the employee polite? Attentive?

How would you judge this salesperson's ability to sell?

Did he/she attempt to cross-sell other items?

How was this person's product knowledge?

Did the store open (or close) on time?

Sometimes the company is pleasantly surprised.

Other times they are stunned by the bad behavior and know exactly why sales are slipping. It's a good system—but like any system, it can be "worked."

John Saccheri owns Mystique Shopper, LLC in Orlando, Florida. He says he has to wind his way through all kinds of flaws in the system.

"It's scary when the company who hires us wants us to create the entire report for them. Or they want to use a report form that is ten or fifteen years old. We have to really work with the company to make sure the survey is relevant and that we are looking for behaviors that can help the company. Otherwise our service has very little value."

Even phrasing the report badly can cause problems.

"Companies will ask us to fill out a report where the customer service ratings are; (1) Wow (2) What I expected, and (3) Less Than I Expected. Well, if you get a "Wow" reaction the first time you went in, great. But, you go in a second time and you know it is going to be great—so you mark down (2) What I expected—because the service was what I expected; great. Skews the outcome, doesn't it? Yes and No are also not very helpful answers. If I go into a store and the questions is, 'Was the employee friendly?' and I answer 'No.' No isn't very helpful. Why? What did he/she do that wasn't friendly? We need a much more descriptive explanation to go with the report."

John says a lot of upper management folks are out of touch.

"We did work for a jewelry chain that built its customer base on being friendly and always offering to clean people's jewelry. The company was famous for that service and upper management just assumed it was always being done. After a long shopping test, we found out that in all of the visits, only one customer was

offered a free jewelry cleaning. Management
couldn't believe it. They took the process for
granted."

And, the employees learn how to work the system, too.
They know they are eventually going to be "shopped" so they
watch for telltale signs. They watch for patterns, Saccheri
says.

"Management will often ask for a planned
sequence of events to happen. They will tell us to
first send our people to the bar for a drink, then
sit down for dinner, and finally visit the dance
club or whatever. Well, employees are smart. They
look for patterns. If they catch on to the pattern,
they will eliminate customers who don't follow the
sequence. It's not a perfect system...pretty
close...but not perfect."

Hess told me that employees are very defensive and
use lots of excuses for not being polite—or for not repeating
the customer's name.

"They will say something like, 'I didn't say their
name because it was a foreign name and I didn't
want to insult them by mispronouncing it.' Or, 'I
didn't know if I should say Mrs. Ms. or Miss so I
didn't say anything. But these are all excuses
and none of them are acceptable."

Some employees fight "the report."
When there is a large bonus attached to an employee's
customer service behavior, you can bet that employees will
fight even harder for their right to blame the customer. Saccheri told me about a car dealership that had a very strict
customer service policy. The procedure was that you; (1) offer

the customer a test drive, (2) offer to appraise their used car, (3) offer to explain all the features of the new car...and about five other "must do" items. When one employee was presented with the shopper report, he vehemently contested it. He got angry and convinced the sales manager that he had, in fact, offered the customer every one of those "must do" items. There was a big bonus riding on the review and he didn't think he was being treated fairly. In fact, he demanded to be "re-shopped." Saccheri related,

> *"Unfortunately, the next time the salesman was* <u>*video*</u>*-shopped. When he was shown, on the tape, that he had forgotten to do several things he was supposed to do, he still asked for a reprieve; citing a number of unrelated excuses. And the sales manager let it go."*

Both Hess and Saccheri told me that good customer service teeters on the shaky shoulders of management—and that many of them just don't "buy into" the program. They don't see customer relations as financially important as it is. *"They are all about getting the operations right."* Hess said. *"Everybody has so much to do and is so busy—and there are so many layers in these big organizations...that even if the CEO says he wants a stronger customer service push, it gets lost by the time it reaches the bottom management rung."*

Saccheri agrees. *"Many of these managers say they want to improve customer service but when they get the results, they are in denial about it because it reflects on them."*

Or, maybe you've had an experience where an employee tried to manipulate you into a good customer service score?

Mine was blatant.

I went to have our Jeep serviced and the service manager shamelessly told me, *"You know, we are judged on our customer service here, so be sure to give us a good rating on the survey they send out later, OK? (whispering) That's how we get raises."* When the survey came, I wrote down how the guy had tried to influence my vote. I never heard a word back from the company.

John Saccheri had a strange personal experience after a particularly good haircut.

> *"When I told the barber that I really liked the haircut he pointed to a small phone number on the bottom of the receipt. 'Great, he said, call this number and tell them. They always like to hear good things'. Now, do you think he would have shown me that phone number if I was an unhappy customer? No way. I'll bet if I called that company to pitch them on my shopping service they would tell me they didn't need it because they have a file full of (only) nice phone calls."*

Both Sacceri and Hess told me the best shift they have seen in their business is that more companies are using shoppers to "catch people doing things right." Companies want the mystery shopper *not* to be viewed as a policeman—but rather a positive part of creating a good customer service culture. When discourteous employees see others being rewarded for good behavior, it makes a strong enough (financial) impression to get them to try being nice.

CHAPTER 14

BIG CHANGE #10 WIN AWARDS...ON PURPOSE

As the winner of several Emmy® Awards and other so-called "recognitions," I know for a fact that your customers look upon you with a great deal more prestige and "standing" than those who don't have them. Furthermore, I attend dozens of corporate award ceremonies each year and I see how the winners are treated by their peers.

They are more credible.

They get more respect..

They are highly pursued by your competition.

They earn more money!

The best thing about the award is that it isn't perceived as self-promotion. Your efforts are being heralded by your industry and by an independent judging committee.

Every industry has awards. Find out as much as you can about past winners and fill out an application, tomorrow.

Get in the game.

Even if you aren't even nominated, for an award, in your first year of entry, make an effort to study who won and why.

Keep submitting your work until you are successful.

When I wanted to be a headliner comedian, booking agents would say, "You need a TV credit...or some national exposure." So, I entered a local comedy contest and finished dead last; from a field of 200 comedians. So, I listened to audio tapes of my stage time. I watched what the successful comedians on *The Tonight Show* were doing. I honed my craft as often as I could. The next year I placed 5th out of 200. The third year, I won first place in the contest and the resulting newspaper and television "exposure" propelled me to headliner status—and eventually my first TV hosting job. Applying the exact same formula resulted in my winning numerous Emmy® awards.

You won't believe what a difference winning awards makes in the area of employee pride. That feeling of individual (or team) pride in your organization streams quickly (and profitably) to your customers.

Maybe you've been in the "ratings" crosshairs of *Consumer Reports*? *AAA*? *The Mobil Travel Guide*? *JD. Powers & Associates*?

What do these ratings mean?

Who can you believe?

More importantly, who can your customers believe?

Well, even if it is misinterpreted—or you have paid to participate in the rating process (ala J.D. Powers & Associates, for example) high ratings can do wonders for your business. They are the equivalent of winning an Oscar® or an Emmy®. When an outsider judges your work and unflinchingly awards you a merited differentiation, customers use that information in their decision making.

Buyers tend to spend more money with a higher rating.

Mobil claims that the difference between a five star hotel rating and a four star rating is $115 a night. ($505 vs. $390). Mobil uses "stars." AAA uses "diamonds."

How do they gather their research?

Most research is done by the equivalent of highly trained secret shoppers; dozens of them. The "inspectors" arrive unannounced, take meticulous notes, and may spend 100 days a year on the road gathering information and filling out 500-item questionnaires. Others use telephone surveys. Yet others, like J.D. Powers, are paid handsome fees by the companies that are being rated; just to be included in the survey. One researcher told me he didn't put a whole lot of stock in their method because they are only "picking the low hanging fruit" and not doing research on the non-paying businesses.

But what *is* valid are the behaviors "the raters" look for.

In the hotel game, for example, high ratings go to hotels who:

- Deliver your bags to your room within 10 minutes of check in

- Deliver wake up calls by a human voice and not a machine

- Deliver a follow-up wake up call by a human voice

- Coffee shop cups are never dry for more than 30 seconds

- A drink is offered within a minute of your glass being empty

- Employees should always use your name

- No scuffs on the walls

- Employees greeting you every time they see you

- Employees escorting you to a location rather than simply pointing you in the right direction

- Sparkling clean silverware at your dinner table

You get points for going above and beyond the call of duty for:

- Offering a bottle of water upon check out

- Getting a freshly washed car from the Valet

- Offering a collection of current magazines upon checkout

HOW DO YOU BECOME THE BEST BANK?

A Consumer Reports Money Advisor study rated Bank of America the best bank in 2004.

The categories they used for this survey included; multi-state convenience of the branch and ATM's, electronic banking, penalty fees for returned checks, "free" checking services, and bank personnel.

Bank of America seems to be hitting on all cylinders.

I did a customer service seminar for Wilshire State Bank in Los Angeles. Wilshire State is a fast growing bank chain that specializes in a largely Korean customer base. One employee touted Bank of America for doing something pretty incredible.

"I was out of gas and out of money so I had to cash a check in a hurry. B of A was the only bank around. The teller noticed (from my driver's license) it was my birthday and said something nice about it. Two days later, I got a birthday card in the mail from the Bank of America with signatures from all the bank employees. I was shocked. I thought, we should be doing that!"

What would lower your rating on the *Consumer Reports* bank survey? For example, points were deducted from U.S Bank because customers had to wait in lobby lines for longer than five minutes.

So if you trust the ratings or not, realize that "the best" are being judged on a pretty high scale. If you plan to be competitive, but don't want to invest tens of thousands of dollars to be included in the J.D. Powers award pool, at least *act* like you did.

LEARN FROM ORGANIZATIONS WHO ARE GETTING IT RIGHT.

CHAPTER 15

THESE ORGANIZATIONS MADE THE BIG CHANGES

The organizations in this chapter "get it."

They love their employees. They empathize with them.

They love their customers. They show empathy towards them.

They realize they must strive to be nimble and relevant because their customers are emotionally charged moving targets. These organizations also take into account how the 911 terrorist attacks changed the world...and the customer.

Since that day, the expectations for great service were irrevocably altered.

When it was known that we were being attacked on our home soil, Americans came to the realization that their lives could be snuffed out in an instant—vaporized before they experienced the amazing things life has to offer. As I've mentioned earlier, people want to feel like they are living for a purpose. They want to squeeze as much out of life as they can; while they're here. That certainly applies to their purchase "experiences." They want to be treated well and believe that the money they spend is going for something special.

Experience seekers want more than the minimum in customer service. They want you to provide valuable information, an education, some entertainment, a pleasant atmosphere, and (if you can do it) a memorable event worth taking pictures of and posting on their personal web sites.

Tom Peters calls this extraordinary experience "Wowing" the customer.

I had one of those.

Maria Garcia was an employee who "Wowed" me at the Orlando Marriott Hotel. Below is the story; which was originally published in *Nobody Moved Your Cheese!*

MARIA GARCIA

I was in Orlando, Florida entertaining at a conference for a large office equipment company. I checked into the Orlando World Center Marriott Hotel; absolutely starving.

I called room service and ordered a cheeseburger and a Diet Coke. When the room service waitress rang my doorbell, she brought in a mouth-watering, mile high cheeseburger and a Diet Pepsi. She said they didn't have any more diet Coke in the kitchen and hoped the Pepsi would be OK. I was polite but told her I was "Jones-ing" for a Diet Coke and asked her to please take the Pepsi back.

She left.

Forty seconds later, my doorbell rang again and the same server is standing there with an ice cold Diet Coke. I said, "I thought you said the kitchen was out of Coke?"

She replied, "We are. But I got this one out of the machine four floors down." I tried to pay her but she wouldn't take my money. She said, "I just want you to be happy at our hotel."

When I regained consciousness, I jumped to the phone to ring the hotel manager. I rattled on and on; bragging about this woman. Then, I asked him for the Marriott International headquarters so I could continue my crusade about this lady. (I'll call her Maria Garcia to preserve her privacy). My cheeseburger got cold, the home fries got rigor mortis—and I didn't even care!

That was customer service of mythic proportions! For the dollar she spent on that Diet Coke, the Marriott won a lifetime customer.

What happened to Maria Garcia? I called about a year later and found out she had been named the food & beverage manager at one of their Northern State properties.

Gee, what a surprise.

By now, I'll bet I've told 200,000 people about Maria Garcia. She was an example of a person who respected how

I felt about my soft drink preference. She left me with an, "I want to stay here again" feeling.

And, I have stayed there again and again; on purpose!

As a result of that outstanding experience, I have become a microphone-toting unpaid salesperson for Maria Garcia and the Marriott hotels—all thanks to one room service attendant who took the initiative to make sure I was a happy customer.

How much publicity can *you* generate for $1.00?

"SMALL" CAN BEAT "BIG" WHEN YOU CARE ABOUT PEOPLE

I hope the following examples will inspire you smaller businesses to exploit building relationships and listening to your customers. You can use your agility to respond more quickly in battling your larger competition. And for you big players, don't underestimate the "little guys." They are gaining on you...unless you behave like:

BOSTON'S/BOSTON PIZZA

George Melville and Jim Treliving bought this small franchise operation in 1983 and have since built the chain to over 200 stores. Their growth has been phenomenal because they are obsessed with every small step of the customer experience. At an International franchisee conference, I heard Boston Pizza International, President, Mark Pacinda, enthusiastically describe the total customer experience this way:

> *"The experience begins the moment your guests approach your front door. The door opens for them and your guests are surprised and delighted to*

be met by a greeter, who welcomes them warmly and immediately leads them to their table. Your guests can't help but notice their table is spotless and perfectly set. They look around and the whole restaurant is clean; immaculate. And that just adds to their growing feeling of comfort. And just as quickly as they settle, their cheerful server arrives to take their drink orders and offer assistance with their menu choices. That server is not only going to answer any question they might have but also invite them to try an add-on or participate in a special promotion, all the while building their anticipation of the delicious food that will soon be arriving. And when those meals arrive, the timing is perfect and the fresh, hot meals exquisitely prepared and masterfully presented. "My God, it looks just like it does in the menu!" Their eyes widen at the sight of this wonderful food, their nostrils fill with the tantalizing aromas, and then they take a bite— perfection. And as they make their way to their car, across your neatly maintained parking lot, they argue. Yeah, argue—about whose idea it was to come to Boston Pizza in the first place. They all want to take the credit."

Because Boston's/Boston Pizza is so concerned about providing the total customer experience before, during, and after the transaction, they can't help but keep growing the franchise at a record pace.

THE WATCH MAN

The Watch Man store in Laughlin, Nevada sells more wristwatches than any other store in the world; some 20,000 every year. What might shock you is that its location isn't very glamorous. *The Watch Man* occupies about 2,000 square feet inside a small, remote casino.

However, size and glamour doesn't matter because *The Watch Man* cares about the feelings of their customers. Usually, when you go to buy a wristwatch, the watches are locked behind glass cases or tall plastic kiosk cylinders. The unspoken assumption is that if the watches were in full view, customers would steal them. At *The Watch Man*, all of the watches are laid out on tables, in the open. The customer automatically thinks, "These people trust me."

The Watch Man's fun starts every morning at 8:50am.

The store opens at 9:00am but there is always a "Spin For Spirit" ten minutes before opening. All of the employees gather around a wheel-of-fortune type wheel and the managers start chanting, *"Watch Man. Watch Man. Rah, Rah, Rah!! "Watch Man.—Watch Man. Rah, Rah, Rah!! Let's go have fun today! Let's sell a lot of watches today!"* The noise is almost deafening—but really infectious. When you are standing outside the locked gate, you feel as if you are missing out on something fun. Then, when the cheering and applause starts to die down, the floodgates open and customers stream inside at full speed. Inside, there are long tables with thousands of watches in full view; not under glass cases. There is a big sign that reads,

> Pick it up. Try it on. If you see one on my wrist that you like, take it off me!

One of the founders, Mack Jett, told me, "It doesn't matter what business you're in, and we have been in a few, our only job is to create customers. We do that by having fun and keeping in mind that we want lifetime employees—which in turn creates lifetime customers."

Notice how Jett said he wanted lifetime employees before he said lifetime customers?

He has the order right. One spawns the other.

The Watch Man founders truly care about their employees. Mack Jett and his partner, Ray Lindstrom, encourage fun ideas for growth at every level of the organization. For example, the watch repair technician also doubles as an Elvis Impersonator twice a day. The operations manager creates cooking contests, offers personal counseling sessions, and organizes company bowling tournaments. Each hour, employees take turns on the store PA system to spin the big "Spirit Wheel" and hand out door prizes to customers. You cannot help but smile when you walk through the door. The grin lasts until after you leave. Maybe it's because they don't say, *"May I help you?"* Instead, they greet you with, *"Are you having fun today?"* Oh, and what about their customer care policy? If you buy a watch and it stops working, they will repair or replace it for free.

No questions. No arguments.

One woman got all the way back to her home in Paris, France and her watch stopped. *The Watch Man* sent her three new wrist watches for free.

CALLAWAY GOLF CLUBS—PART DEUX

When I read the "Jake story" in *Trading up*, I thought of my brother-in-law, Matt Dale. He is a high school basketball coach who isn't pulling down CEO wages. But in golf, he's got "game." Matt played golf in high school and can tell the difference between various "sets of sticks." So, he proudly plays with a set of $3,000 dollar Callaway's. I'm sure they are great clubs but Callaway has a unique way of making the customer feel important and singular. You can actually visit their Carlsbad, California headquarters for a custom fitting before you buy. They will analyze every element of your swing. They will gauge your angle of strike, your club head speed, and how far you hit the ball. When your analysis is over, you get a document from the company—that you then take to an authorized dealer who will "fill the prescription" for you. After an experience like that, I dare you to try to get a golfer to hit a ball with any other clubs.

THE MUSIC EXPERIENCE PROJECT

Music is already an emotional experience for most people. But this museum tribute to rock music sweeps you back in time...a time that stirs up your worst prom dates, your first love, your first car, and so on. The whole building is designed around how music has made you feel.

Microsoft co-founder, Paul Allen, loved Jimi Hendrix (a fellow Pacific Northwest native) so much that he wanted to build a dedicated museum to Jimi in Seattle, Washington. When Jon Magnusson, President of the Magnusson/Klemencic structural engineering firm, first met with Paul to talk about the project, he could tell this was about a rock fan being able to live out his dream. Says Jon,

> *"Paul was so excited about this project that he was willing to spend $30 million dollars to make it a reality. But the more he talked about it—like a little kid—the more he got fired up. Until finally, Paul decided he would create more than a monument to Jimi Hendrix. Paul wound up spending over $240 million to create a total music "theme park."*

So what's the big deal about this place?

First of all, it's totally interactive. You can touch and play with everything. You'll be overwhelmed by the three story tall "tornado" made entirely of electric and acoustic guitars. The laser light show concert hall is fantastic for live performances. You can visit several costume museum rooms filled with stage uniforms worn by your favorite stars of rock & roll, grunge, and the blues. There are sophisticated mini recording studios where you can walk in, play an instrument, record yourself, and burn your creation to a CD. Or, you can just soak up the impossibility of the building. The building's structure is an unforgettable free form design by architectural genius, Frank Gehry. Because of the countless sweeping curves and disappearing roof lines, the exposed interior ribbing gives you the feeling of being swallowed by a gargantuan prehistoric creature. The building has been called, "A black box in a voluptuously undulating musical form" and "the most beautifully ugly building in the Pacific Northwest."

Because of all the sights and sounds enveloping you, you can get lost in your past here.

Who wouldn't find that emotional?

Who wouldn't tell their friends about it?

MIKE DIAMOND PLUMBING

What can a plumber do to change the way you feel about hiring a plumber?

If your home floods or the toilet backs up, you just want it fixed, right? If you're a plumber, how can you differentiate your plumbing business from all the others? Well, in Southern California, *Mike Diamond Plumbing* listened to what plumbing customers wanted and found a way to deliver a unique plumbing experience.

His marketing campaign is brilliantly simple.

"We promise our plumbers will show up on time and smell good."

What more could you want from your plumber? Imagine not having to tie up your day during a 2–3 hour window of time—only to have a stinky plumber walk away; trailing grease on your floors. With Mike's service, your home looks cleaner than when he arrived.

You can imagine how quickly word-of-mouth spreads for Mike Diamond and his business. All he had to do was listen to the complaints he'd heard from his competition's unhappy customers.

LUCKY STRIKE BOWLING LANES

Bowling alleys are on the endangered entertainment list.

In so many towns across America (in the 50's, 60's and early 70's) the local bowling alley was, for adults, a weekly social event. My mom used to bowl in a weekly league—as did everyone else in our neighborhood. The few times I went along, the lanes were packed with colorfully embroidered silk shirts, spilled beer, and deadly serious amateur "rollers."

But in the past 20 years, bowling lane operators have watched league play dwindle from 6 nights a week to one night a week, if that. A couple who works full time simply can't commit the time anymore. And if they do have a free night, they have a lot of other choices. Some bowling owners have been forced to abandon league bowling altogether. They're attracting bowlers with gimmicks like Cosmic Bowling (black lights & lasers), .99 cent lane nights, video game rooms, and "bumper bowling." Bumper bowling is a fence-like device that actually pops up and blocks the ball from going into the gutters. That way, youngsters can learn to roll the ball—and hit the pins—without dumping all those gutter balls. I really like this innovation. With bumper bowling, lane operators have eliminated the customer-killing emotions of embarrassment and humiliation.

However, the most outrageous, next-generation, bowling lane chain has listened to what caused this cultural icon to erode—and provided an alternative.

At we go to print, *Lucky Strike Lanes* has eleven locations and are changing the entire bowling alley "experience." They promote themselves as "America's First Bowling Lounge." Each location boasts a 40-foot tall exterior wall mural of a sexy woman caressing a bowling ball. The front entrance looks more like a night club than a bowling alley. Inside, the look is also…well uh…sexy. There is a trendy looking sports bar area with plasma TV's. Off to one side is a private four lane bowling area set up for parties. The main lanes are outfitted with large, comfy lounge chairs and couches instead of the old hard fiberglass bucket seats. The scoreboard is a 42" plasma monitor that automatically calculates all the scores for you. No more broken pencils and tough 10th frame arithmetic. The "artwork" on the projection screen walls, behind the pins, displays sports bar friendly images. Then, after 10 p.m. the artwork changes to reflect a more adult mood. Sex and the city goes bowling.

And, the food is great.

The first tip off is that Lucky Strike doesn't sell nachos with the liquid cheese option. In fact, they've hired real chefs at each location.

Do they make money?

Compare this: While some lane operators are scrambling to fill up their .99 cent lane night, Lucky Strike Lanes might sell out the whole "club" for $40,000 a night. Corporations and publicity companies are using Lucky Strike Lanes for everything from wedding receptions to movie premiers.

When a cultural shift takes place within your customer base, (i.e. their interests and habits change) only fools live in denial.

Winners profit by remaining relevant.

SADDLEBACK CHURCH

In 1980, Pastor Rick Warren went door to door and surveyed neighbors in Lake Forest, California. He wanted to know what people liked and disliked about going to church.

He listened carefully and changed the entire church-going experience.

These days, Saddleback attracts a non-denominational congregation of 30–40,000 to their beautiful 120 acre college campus-like compound; on a holiday weekend.

And, he does all of this without a television show!

Rick's book, *Purpose Driven Life,* which sells about a million copies per month worldwide, has been recognized as, *"The bestselling hardback nonfiction book in history."* Today more than 350,000 church leaders from 120 countries have been trained in the Purpose-Driven paradigm.

Forbes magazine says, *"Were it a business, Saddleback church would be compared with Dell, Google or Starbucks."* *Time* magazine called Rick Warren, *"America's most influential pastor."*

Saddleback Church received a lot of press when a young Atlanta woman, Ashley Smith, was abducted by murder suspect, Brian Nichols. Ms. Smith read passages from *Purpose Driven Life,* and her captor felt compelled to release her.

The Saddleback "experience" starts on the lush driveway entering the campus. The ever smiling parking staff pleasantly guides you to five convenient parking lots. "Greeters" shake your hand and say "Hello" as you walk through the campus to the various worship centers. You can hear the music pumping from a quarter mile away.

In fact, creativity is a core element of Saddleback's success. Rick Muchow, Justin Adams and their creative arts team have attracted some of California's best musicians and vocalists to perform at each service. You can sit in the main worship center and watch Rick Warren roam the stage. Or, you can soak up the southern California sunshine in an outdoor café and watch the service on large viewing monitors.

Saddleback bills itself as "the church for the unchurched" and it works so well because they have listened to their "customers." They know that not all people want the same thing. At Saddleback, the main worship center holds about 3,000 people per service. If that's not your style, there are many other worship venues on the grounds. There is a building that features a Hawaiian service, with island music. Another, called "Overdrive," caters to the rock and roll crowd. The "Praise" venue has a traditional gospel feel. And, there is a Spanish service called "El Encuentro" (The encounter). On top of that, Saddleback has a High School ministry and two dozen Sunday school classrooms. The campus boasts a bookstore, a volleyball sand lot, and a terraced amphitheater. Furthermore, to prove they are dedicated to this community, Saddleback offers enough free classes to fill a Junior college catalog. Classes to help recovering substance abusers, sexual abusers, classes for married couples, single people, classes on parenting, separated men classes, and the list goes on. To say that the Saddleback experience is emotional is an understatement. The entire "experience" imbues a feeling of a community taking care of itself—healing itself when necessary.

Successful, yes. But at the core of any church's ongoing popularity are the pastors and their consistent delivery of the "product."

This ain't your Daddy's church.

First of all, Rick Warren isn't a televangelist.

He isn't a fire-and-brimstone $2,000 Italian suit wearing preacher. And, he isn't wearing a Nehru jacket or a laying-on-hands to heal you kind of guy. He's big and jolly and wears Hawaiian shirts. His humor is self deprecating. He's topical and relevant as he casually weaves in the events of the past week. And, when he's not speaking (due to his heavy travel schedule) his fellow teaching pastors Glen Kruen, Tom Holladay, Doug Fields, Lance Witt and Gerald Sharon deliver the same unusually fun experience.

Rick says, *"We want you to be able to say that what we talked about on the weekend gave you something that could help you on Monday: in your family, at your work, with your life."*

It works.

Regardless of the religion or faith you subscribe to...or if you don't believe in one at all...this is a social phenomenon worth noticing. It's certainly a phenomenon *your customers* are noticing. The success of Saddleback is a testimony to what can happen when you listen to your customers—*before* they start shouting back.

THE PUBLIC UTILITY "EXPERIENCE"

I've been surprised to get calls to speak to power companies like Touchstone Energy, Southern California Edison, Florida Power and Light, East Kentucky Power Cooperative, and others.

Why would a company who has a virtual monopoly on selling public power care about providing good customer service? As one employee told me, *"We have to be nice to our residential customers because we are the last bill they pay every month."* Public utilities also want to inoculate their culture (to dispense good will) in case government regulations radically change their business models.

They saw what happened to the Cable TV companies.

Remember how abused you were by the Cable TV companies when they had a lock on the Pay-TV business? The Cable TV operators were pretty cocky for awhile. Service was abominable.

They underestimated the sleepy little Satellite TV entities.

Well, when TV customers had a choice, they shouted back.

Cable TV companies forgot that customer demand always determines the ebb and flow of money into the market.

When cable customers got tired of bad service, high prices, and waiting half a day to get hooked up, millions of people switched to Satellite boxes. A company like *Dish Networks* can offer local, national, and global programming at extremely competitive prices.

Now, cable companies are forced to be nice.

SPARLING ENGINEERS

This Seattle, Washington based firm specializes in enormously complicated electrical engineering solutions. Their nationally recognized award winning projects range from complex communication applications in hospitals and libraries—to design-and-build solutions for extreme sound and lighting applications.

The folks at Sparling know that most customers think of engineers as staid and uptight—maybe even a little inflexible—certainly not creative in the traditional sense. But Sparling changes that "customer perception" from the first peek at their stationery.

If you were to judge the wild logo artwork on their web site or their stationery, you would assume the company was the advertising firm for MTV or an avant-garde fashion designer. Here is just one sample of what I'm talking about.

When I first got a letter from them, I couldn't stop staring because I was trying to figure out what all those odd shaped people and colorful characters meant! (www.sparling.com)

CEO Jim Duncan told me,

"We get a lot of great reactions from our clients, especially new clients, who have an expectation that we are very different from other engineering firms; which we are. We don't talk or act like your typical engineers. Our customers have told us they want to be able to talk to human beings; not technical wizards. We work hard teaching our new engineers how to communicate like human beings. And our clients appreciate it. We take pride in living up to our image of being a little bit wild...and people like that."

Judging from the large number of prestigious awards I've seen them win, Jim is being humble. Their clients love them.

SOMEBODY ELSE SELLS COFFEE?

It is nearly impossible to find a street corner in America that hasn't sprouted a *Starbucks* coffee shop. There are plenty of copycats but most people gravitate to the well known brand because they know what to expect.

I am not a gravitator.

I like to see what the competition is doing. On a trip to Portland, Oregon, for the *Oregon Bankers Association*, I ducked into a small coffee shop, on Salmon Street, called *Coffee People.*

The 20-ish man behind the counter, Jason, was tall, blond, and grinned at me as his voice boomed. *"How are you doing, brother?"* he grinned. I asked him for a regular coffee and he said, *"That's good, but could I persuade you to try the peppermint? It's tons better. And if you don't like it, I promise I will pour it all over that guy* (pointing to a male co-worker). As he's pouring my coffee, Jason was humming tunes and saying hello to everyone in line—like he'd known them for years. When a woman walked in and whimpered, *"Oh I missed out on all the chocolate chip cookies,"* Jason shot back, *"How sad for you. But don't reach for the Prozac. I've got some more in the fridge."* His co-worker tried to stop him. *"No, I think I already put out the last box."* Jason insisted, *"Humor me. The fridge is evil and can be very deceptive. But I know how to handle her. (Now, back to us) I'd appreciate it if you would all stand here and hold your breath until I get back."* He disappeared through a swinging door and bounced back out with a fresh box of cookies. *"It was tough fight but you all are worth it."*

The entire coffee shop was laughing, now.

Jason is a good example how just one infectious personality can make buying a cup of coffee an emotional event.

As I was about to leave, a customer came in and asked, "Do you guys sell *Naked Juice?*" Jason said, *"Yeah, but I need to warn you, its way more juice than naked."*

I'd buy my coffee there every day if I lived in Portland.

EL CAJON HARLEY DAVIDSON

My friend, Rand, bought a new motorcycle from El Cajon Harley Davidson, near San Diego. But before he rode it home, he wanted to have some extra chrome and accessories installed; which is a common affliction for most Harley buyers. It was going to take a few days to attach the new goodies so we planned a "break in" ride for the weekend.

Two days later, my friend woke up in a cold sweat; worried.

Rand couldn't remember seeing the "EFI" signature on the air cleaner. EFI stands for Electronic Fuel Injection. So, now he thinks he bought a carbureted bike instead. A model he didn't want. He also knows the shop may have started putting accessories on the wrong motorcycle. So, he calls the dealer and says, *"I think we may have a problem..."* The dealer interrupted him to say, *"Let me reassure you, whatever it is, there is no problem. Everything's going to be fine."* The store's willingness to make sure there was no difficulty immediately calmed Rand's fears. And, he was convinced that he'd bought from the right company.

WEST MARINE

Last March, I met Chuck Hawley, Vice President of Product Development for the 218-store *West Marine Boat*

Supply chain. West Marine sells every kind of recreational and industrial boating equipment imaginable. Chuck told me, *"We have a Zero-Ten philosophy. We only sell merchandise with zero defects—and we insist on providing 10% better service than our customers expect."* As a fan of power boating, I've spent more than my monthly allowance in pursuit of my boating habits...and I have never had a problem buying (or returning) something at a West Marine store. Chuck also told me that he instructs his people, *"Don't shop with your own wallet."*

What does that mean?

Boating equipment is expensive—and some sales associates may feel uncomfortable showing a high priced item to a customer. Chuck drives home the point that salespeople should never pre-judge the customer's intentions or their buying power. For boat owners, price is secondary if the item is a piece of lifesaving equipment or navigation gear. Boaters are never afraid to pay a higher price for safety. One of the funniest things I'd ever heard said about sailing was, *"Being in the hull of a sailboat in high seas is like being in jail with the possibility of drowning."*

Money is no object when it comes to keeping the deck side up.

Chuck, who is an award winning sailor, says customer feedback is the main reason they lead the industry.

> *"We are constantly putting our products through difficult sea trials. If we get a new piece of gear we take it on the water ourselves. If it fails or doesn't live up the brand's promise, we go back to the vendor and ask for improvements. We constantly ask customers for their feedback. If they tell us a product's performance is lacking in one area or another, we either drop the line or*

*correct it immediately. For example, we've been
very influential in making huge changes in some
of the navigational electronics because we
respect our customer's real water experiences
and want other boat owners to get the very best
from us."*

Don't you wish you could get the same customer dedication from your dry cleaner, your grocery store, your hair salon, your auto dealer, and your bank?

You can...if you speak up when the right people are listening.

STATE BANK

State Bank is a regional chain of (20) banks, based in La Grange, Texas. Keeping a finger on the pulse of their customer's changing needs is paramount to the growth of this company.

President and CEO, L. Don Stricklin and his team empower each employee to make the big decisions in the best interest of the customer. But, they are also sensitive to the little things that are so meaningful to their customers. State Bank knows that a lot of customers rush straight from work to their bank—only to find the doors locked. So, State bank has a policy to open the bank 5 minutes before the posted time. And, they close the bank 5 minutes later than the posted time.

Want a loan? State Bank can process all consumer loan applications within one hour. Can your bank do that?

Each person updates their voice mail daily so that customers know somebody is on the job...today! If you call for information—and they cannot answer the phone—someone will call you back within 4 hours. Problem resolution is taken care of within 24 hours.

Everybody wears a name badge to sanction account-ability.

And, saying *"Thank You"* is a rewarded behavior.

In business, banking has got to be one of the hardest in which to turn a profit. And small regional banks are always takeover targets. Don doesn't worry about that stuff. He worries about the customers. In fact, he told me that (in banking circles) a 50% expense to revenue ratio is what the stock pickers look for. State Bank's expenses are closer to 70%.. But Don believes they will continue to win, because the expenses are related to retaining customers.

If you were their customer, wouldn't you agree?

EYEMART EXPRESS

Dr. Doug Barnes was the first person I ever heard use the expression, "Our goal is to out-friendly the competition."

Apparently, so do his customers. Since opening his first store June 11th, 1990, *Dr. Barnes Eyemart Express* has grown to 65 retail stores—turning in $75 million in sales. Barnes told me their success is based on two simple ideas; (1) get the prescription right the first time, and (2) out-friendly the competition.

Doug Barnes was an Optometrist who discovered new patients were coming to him complaining that they had to update their eyeglass prescriptions; almost annually. Barnes said, *"Eyes don't deteriorate that quickly. The problem was they weren't getting the right prescription the first time."* So, he opened a small eyewear store in Appleton, Wisconsin, to prove his point. Today, his stores, Eyemart Express, Vision4Less, Eyewear Express, and VisionMart Express span 15 states. Barnes also prides himself on being able to offer 1-hour service and the ability *"to beat any name brand frame price or it's free."* That's impressive considering his name brand competition is Lens Crafters, Eyemasters, and Pearle Vision . Barnes says, *"We're not as big but we can always out-friendly those guys. We hire from within the community so our people know their customers. How can the big guys compete with that?"*

They also do something incredibly unique with their pricing.

At this writing, (prices may change by the time you read this) you can visit an Eyemart Express and get a pair of single vision eyeglasses for $38.74. Or, you can but two pair for $67.92, $98.61, and $138.74. Want bifocals? They're priced at $108.61 for two pair.

Do you see what they're doing, here?

Eyemart isn't pricing their products at the terribly-over-used $39.95, and $69.95 price points. By "off-pricing" there is the perception that these prices have been squeezed down to the last penny of acceptable profit.

Doug Barnes, and his senior management team, also impressed me as executives who care as much about their employees as they do their customers. I got a chance to meet all 65 store managers at their annual retreat. Doug flew the entire management team to Las Vegas for three days; all expenses paid.

This wasn't to be an intense sales meeting or trade show.

This trip was to reward the managers for a job well done and to let them blow off a little steam. We played an Eyemart History Game Show and Dr. Barnes gleefully handed out $100 bills (to the contestants) for marginally correct answers!

This kind of generosity isn't taken for granted. The managers I talked to loved this job. And, why wouldn't they? They truly believe the company philosophy is in the customer's best interest. Plus, 38% of their employees partici-pate in their generous 401–K plan (they match .75 cents for every dollar). And, even more employees quality than partic-ipate! In addition to the 401K, in 2004, Eyemart Exress paid more than 2 million in incentives.

A lot of high powered, big-company executives could learn something else from Barnes.

He isn't shy about admitting his mistakes.

"We bought a small chain of stores in Puerto Rico and it was a disaster. It lost money from day one. We didn't under-stand how to market it and it's now become the company punch line. Boy, I had a really bad idea down there."

Smart employees know times can be difficult. But simple honesty, integrity and recognition build trust. And, trust has translated into lifetime employees and lifetime cus-tomers for the Eyemart Express stores.

IS THIS THE FRIENDLIEST TOWN IN AMERICA?

Thankfully, there are pockets of small towns that still pride themselves on friendly, personal service. The attitudes in these towns are so pervasive that a whole town can become an emotional experience.

For me, of all the towns, cities, burgs, and burbs I've visited, Wooster, Ohio wins the title of *Friendliest Town in America.*

It really caught me off guard.

Wooster (proudly pronounced Wuss-ter by the locals) is about 50 minutes southwest of Cleveland. Leaving Cleve-land International airport, it only takes ten minutes for buildings to evaporate and be replaced by broad parcels of farm land. At night, it's a bit unsettling because there are no gas stations, no mom and pop diners, no phone booths, not even (dare I say it?) a *Starbucks* in view for 45 long minutes.

Then when you least expect it, in this mid-January ride, just over a small hill, a few sparse lights flickered off the snowy little town of Wooster.

Stop me before I break into a Laura Ingalls-Wilder novel!

Why was I there in mid-January? I had a speaking engagement at the Wooster Chamber of Commerce.

Mark and Sue Peeples picked me up from the Cleveland International airport at 9 p.m. Sue works for the Chamber and her husband, Mark, manages three franchised pizza stores. Both of them are really pleasant folks who gave up a weeknight evening with their children to truck me in from the airport. Immediately considerate, they asked if I was hungry. I said, *"Starving. But I'll just get room service at the hotel."* Mark countered with, *"I suppose you stay in a lot of hotels that have room service. Where you're staying (the Ameri-Host) doesn't. Let's stop at a restaurant."* To make it easy I suggested we go through the Burger King drive up window.

Mark pulls up to the Order Board. An excited, easy to understand adolescent male voice says, "Hi and welcome to Burger King. What can I get for you this evening?" (Typing it doesn't do his *tone* justice. Suffice it to say that nobody has imparted so much hope and enthusiasm in repeating the most oft-recited line in fast food history) I order a #3 with a Diet Coke. We barely make the slight left turn from the Order Board to the first take out window and there is a long, skinny arm protruding into our drive path with my soda. The smiling boy with the Coke says, *"Would you mind pulling ahead to wait for your food?"* We put the car in Drive and pull forward eight feet. But before Mark can even stop the vehicle, the clerk bounds out the front door with our bag of food...blurting, *"Sorry for the delay."*

I haven't been in Wooster four minutes and already I love this place.

Next up, the hotel without room service.

The twenty-something female desk clerk made me feel like I was a visiting Potentate. *"We have been expecting you, Mr. Shafer. How was your flight in? Have you found something to eat?"*

What's funny is that I am no longer tired from the trip. In fact, I feel uncharacteristically energized. As soon as I get to my room, the phone rings. It's Ms. Desk Clerk again. *"Just checking to see if your room is all right...because if it isn't I would happy to move you to another one."* I assured her the room was perfect and thanked her for her thoughtfulness.

OK, this was a nice, late night first impression but tomorrow I'll have some time to snoop around town and check out some other establishments; anonymously.

After a great night's sleep, the clock radio alarm blares. It's 8 a.m.

First stop, McDonalds. I had other choices but I am a total sucker for their bacon, egg & cheese biscuit. A kindly woman, 50-ish, greeted me with, *"What can I get you, hon."* I usually don't like the "hon" bit because it presumes familiarity. But, in record time, Linda V. delivers my meal and stuns me with, *"It's fresh and hot. See you tomorrow!"* See me tomorrow? I've NEVER heard that in my life. She assumed I would be back. Or, maybe it was a clever subliminal message most people don't catch consciously. Regardless, she had spun this invitation so artfully that I felt truly obligated to stay in Wooster an extra day!

I finished my meal and noticed a Wal-Mart across the street. The snow was starting to fall and buying a snuggly stocking cap would be a productive excuse to venture inside. So, I darted through the parking lot to Wooster's main department store. This Wal-Mart had something akin to no other Wal-Mart; a hitching post—with a real life horse and buggy tied up. Yes. A horse and buggy; peacefully coexisting amongst Ford Pickups and Nissan Altimas. Until now, it hadn't occurred to me that we were close enough to Pennsylvania that there would be a strong Amish–Wal-Mart–shopping contingent in the farm lands of Wooster. In this community, Wal-Mart was doing its civic best to accommodate all preferred modes of transportation.

> *SIDE STORY: I also learned from Sue and Mark that there have been incidents in Wooster where Amish carriage drivers have been pulled over by the local police to be awarded a DUI (Driving while Under the Influence) citation. While alcohol is forbidden by their religion, a few "mavericks" have been known to take more than a snort, fire up the buggy, pass out, and run into the police cars who were trying to stop them. And, how about this. It turns out that Amish teenagers are like teenagers everywhere. They're apparently peer bound to disobey their parents. Mark said that it isn't uncommon for a group of Amish kids to pool their milk money and buy a car. Then they hide it in the woods along with "normal" clothes, and sneak out for some Anti-Amish joy riding. "It's in the paper all the time." Mark said. He explained that their out-of-character reveling can get sideways pretty fast and the ensuing fender benders invariably blow their cover. I couldn't help but wonder how many Amish teens bore secret tattoos.*

Back to the Wal-Mart.

The same moment I found a nice watchman's cap, my ears tuned into the overheard PA announcer telling us about a sale in their toy department. But this announcer was not a "pro." His regular-guy tone of voice and loose "script" sounded as if he was offering a kind gesture; not a pitch. "Hi everybody." He said. *"I don't know if you have a birthday coming up for the kids or not...but if you do, check out our toy department where we have a lot of fun items on our promotional shelf. You really ought to stop by if you're in a pinch for a gift. Thank you for shopping your Wooster Wal-Mart S-U-PE-R Center!"*

Wow. I'm a trained broadcaster but I paled by comparison.

This was a concerned neighbor talking to other neighbors. That's by far the most trusted method to sell anything. I never met this man but I would swear on a stack of Ohio travel brochures that this man was a native Woosterian.

One last stop.

I must have left my favorite pen on the plane so, spotting a nearby *Staples* office supply, I hiked over a snowy berm and ducked through their door. Removing my cap, I combed my hair with my fingers and looked up to see an elderly man sternly coming toward me bearing a name badge that read, ED. Ed looked over his glasses and said, *"Unless I miss my guess you need some office supplies."*

Ed was a pro!

He walked toward me. He greeted me. He was funny. He had my full attention. And I laughed out loud; promising to buy every pen I will ever need in my life...from Ed.

Everywhere I went, the same scenario repeated itself. Nice people eager to interrupt their day to help me find a bookstore, a good cup of coffee, or detailed directions to the town's singular Internet café. A greasy overall wearing truck mechanic sporting an 8" hunting knife strapped to his leg confided in me. "It don't really qualify as a caf-fay but nobody has the guavas to tell 'em,"

After getting dressed for the event, I was picked up at the hotel by the Wooster Chamber Executive Director & High School Football Referee, Mike Lezak. After a few moments with Mike, I realized why my Wooster experience had been so inclusive. Mike told me that in a town of 26,000 (including cows, chicken, and pigs—Mike's words—not mine) more than 800 business people were expected to attend the Gala annual dinner. By comparison, I spoke for the Seattle, Washington Chamber of Commerce (a city of 2 million plus) and only 190 people showed up.

These business people care about their businesses and their community. They band together and they support each other.

That evening the food at the meeting was spectacular. Really!

I mean it was hot, delicious, and beautifully prepared for 800 hungry people. Some had the filet mignon. I had the salmon; which was juicy and absolutely fresh. Now, how do they pull that off during a Central Ohio winter? Because, they care about doing a good job for the people who know them. These chefs are accountable to these people—their friends—in Wooster. Not to be snooty, but I've stayed in the nation's most revered hotels—doing programs for the biggest companies in the world. But I swear, the chefs in some of these 4–5 star hotels could learn a thing or two from the caterers in Wooster.

In fact, every business should all have to set up camp, intern, and learn how to operate a business in Wooster, Ohio. Here in Wooster, courtesy, accountability and taking responsibility for your actions is as natural as breathing.

Granted, Wooster is isolated. There isn't another major town for 40–50 miles. So, if you are living in Wooster, you are probably working in somewhere in Wayne county. You see people you know every day. They do your dry cleaning, prepare your taxes, fix your lawn mower, pray for you if your father is sick, and show up for your daughter's dance recital; not because they have to but because they want to.

Oh, I almost forgot to mention that each place setting was accented by a really nice ceramic navy blue candy dish. Each dish was filled with rich chocolate candies hidden beneath the fitted top. In gold script, each dish was tastefully engraved with the letters CCJ. Later in the evening, Daniel Plumly, the president of the law firm, *Critchfield, Critchfield, and Johnson, Ltd.*, invited everyone to take home their individual candy dishes. Dan announced, *"If you eat all of the candy please come by anytime for a free refill."* Who wouldn't use a lawyer who kept you in free Godiva chocolates?! After dinner, I asked Dan if anybody ever took him up on his offer. He looked at me as if I was daft. *"Yeah, everybody does."* He told me their candy refills are famous. Whenever a client or prospective client drops by they bring their empty dish.

I asked Sue if there was a downside to living in Wooster. She said, *"Uh yeah. The gossip can be pretty rampant. Like most small towns, everybody knows everybody else and can get into your business. People can get a little snoopy."*

Well, if that is the worst sin this town has to offer, I'm in. Hillary Clinton's book, *It Takes A Village* should have profiled this town. As a parent, I don't mind if other parents are aware...or even snooping around my children and their activities. Besides, when it comes to gossip, a lack of fuel extinguishes every fire.

By comparison, for three years, I lived in Woodland Hills, California; a close in suburb of Los Angeles. It was nice neighborhood but most people drove in and out of their electric garage doors; never talking to anybody. I made several attempts to get to know my next door neighbors. No luck. I couldn't even find people to baby-sit my two young boys. So, throw me back to a time when neighbors "keep an eye out" and I'm in heaven.

The morning following my speech to the Chamber, I had to leave Wooster at 5 a.m. to catch a plane to Dallas for another program. I was sad to leave such a warm, friendly, quaint little town where the values of being kind and helpful still meant something. I was even sadder that I was forced to depart before McDonalds opened.

Linda V, please forgive me. I'll be back for a Quarter Pounder another day.

CHAPTER 16

SOME TOUGH QUESTIONS FOR YOU

Creating and retaining lifetime customers is rough work.

It takes time, energy, and boundless patience because in the early stages of developing a customer relationship, the relationship is fragile. They don't know you. You don't know them. And, it requires a few transactions for the customer to feel comfortable about establishing a trusting relationship with you. Then, you have to be able to handle a few bumps in the road if the customer gets mad at you.

So, on your way to building a lasting association, don't blow it. Each interaction either enhances the relationship or degrades it.

It is important that we instill an attitude in our work-force that we are grateful for every customer who shops our stores, orders from our websites, or hires our services. We need to celebrate their existence, their enthusiasm, and their willingness to go out of the way (in a sea of choices) to do business with us. These customers are making our house payments, sending our kids to college, and giving our lives purpose.

ASK YOURSELF THESE TOUGH QUESTIONS:

If your sales are dipping or you are losing market share, don't live on the blind hope that things will get better. In this market, if you are not growing you are shrinking. You need to ask yourself these tough questions:

Do you love your employees enough to put them in the right job?

Do you put them in a job that exploits their true talents and gives them a sense of purpose?

Are you hiring by their resume or by their humanity?

Do you encourage your employees to create a relationship—with your customers—that will eventually lead to emotional loyalty?

Do you *really* love your customers?

Do you know who they are? Single? Married? Children? Interests?

Are you truly grateful your customers chose to spend their time and money with you? How do you show them?

Are you training people to recognize your customer's emotions—even before they say a single word?

What can you do to make customers feel less vulnerable before, during, and after the transaction?

Are you careful about the words you choose and the negative affect some of those words can have on your co-workers and your customers?

Do you evaluate customers more by what they tell you rather than the way they fill out your evaluation forms or answer your surveys?

Can you put aside your own "bad day" to remember it's about the customer and not about *you*?

How can you create a memorable wall-to-wall experience for your customers—in person, on the phone, and over the Internet?

Is the customer's *final moment* with you positive and memorable?

What can you do to create an associative memory for your customers?

Take all the time you need to answer...as long as you attack the above list with urgency.

In the meantime, behave as if your future depends upon it.